Praise for *The Grass Is Greener Right Here*

"David Ault has written a beautiful book showing the boundless ways gratitude can be expressed even through what appears to be life's various hardships. I so enjoyed reading *The Grass is Greener Right Here*, and I know you will too."

> Louise Hay, founder of Hay House
> and author of *You Can Heal Your Life*

"With a heart of generosity and vulnerability, David Ault offers his readers a most trustworthy and indispensable guide for opening wider one's own heart of compassion, courage, and trust. With profound insight derived from his own down-to-earth experiences, David leads us into the discovery that all along the grass in our inner and outer life has been vibrantly green. Breathe often, and let this nourishing and healing book bless your heart."

> Michael Bernard Beckwith, author of *Life Visioning*

"When Mahatma Gandhi stated 'My life is my message,' David Ault's soul was listening. When you read this book you may be captivated by the authenticity and unconditional love David extends to you. That is because his life really is his message. David is a master teacher and storyteller who writes courageously from his heart with absolute transparency. As you read *The Grass Is Greener Right Here*, allow David to be your guide and trust where he beckons you to follow. If you do you'll come to realize you are on an exquisite journey to the most sacred place you have ever been. Paradoxically speaking, it's also the place you never really left; your oneness with Life. Your greatest Good has been right here all along awaiting your return . . . the grass really is greener right where you are."

> Dennis Merritt Jones, author of
> *Your (Re)Defining Moments – Becoming Who You Were Born to Be*

"*The Grass is Greener Right Here* is a beautiful guide to living fully right where you are. Filled with stories and wisdom, this book will break your heart wide open. David Ault has lived these truths and is the perfect guide to experiencing all that life has to offer. Don't miss this book!"

Joel Fotinos, author of *My Life Contract*

"David Ault loves humanity. He has written a book that from the very first words tell poignant stories of that love in a powerful and engaging way. Through heart-opening accounts of humankind's ability to hope in the midst of bleak circumstances, he inspires us to consider the magnificence of being exactly where we are, doing whatever we are doing, and striving for whatever our heart is reaching for. He teaches us to look inward softly and to appreciate the ability we have to love and help one another and ourselves. This is a book of profound inspiration."

Edward Viljoen, author of *The Power of Meditation*

"David Ault's latest work, *The Grass Is Greener Right Here*, is masterfully written, displaying both passion and compassion and inspiring each of us to grow, expand, and reassess what we hold as priorities. *The Grass Is Greener Right Here* emphasizes that perception is the ultimate reality, but not necessarily the ultimate truth."

Bishop Carlton Pearson, author of *The Gospel of Inclusion*

"In *The Grass Is Greener Right Here*, David Ault takes us on an exhilarating journey that touches the heart, dares us to think, and anchors these insights with questions that inspire each of us to look inward for our own answers. For anyone on the path of self-discovery, this book is a must read!"

Karen Drucker, recording artist and author of *Let Go of the Shore*

"David Ault's newest work, *The Grass Is Greener Right Here*, never talks down to its readers. It rapturously takes them higher. Through David's own experiences of adjusting perception and reclaiming truth, he offers a helping hand by asking the questions that deliver us to healing and happiness. *The Grass Is Greener Right Here* is spiritual truth. You won't want to put it down."

David Kessler, author of *Life Lessons* with Elisabeth Kubler Ross and *You Can Heal Your Heart* with Louise Hay

ALSO BY DAVID AULT

Where Regret Cannot Find Me

The Joyful Journey of Mindfulness (e-book)

The Grass Is Greener Right Here

We Are What We See

David Ault

RUN TO THE ROAR
PUBLISHING

THE GRASS IS GREENER RIGHT HERE

Run to the Roar Publishing

Editing and Layout by Words of Passion

Copyright © 2014 by David Ault

ISBN: 978-0692321973

This book was printed in the United States of America.

Dedication

This book is dedicated to Louise Hay, my first teacher, whose profound example of living spiritual principles changed the direction of my life. Thank you for guiding me down the road of self-love and ceaselessly encouraging me to blaze a new trail of unconformity and adventure.

Contents

The Grass Is Greener Right Here

> You get there by realizing you are already there.
>
> — Eckhart Tolle

Sitting on the wooden crate, I gaze at the shadows that darken the thatched walls of the hut. In my arms is the squirming, restless body of a young boy, perhaps five or six years of age, whose underdeveloped neck muscles fail to hold his head upright.

Cerebral palsy, I guess, observing his lack of functioning motor skill coordination. His older sister watches cautiously while I hold him. She cannot attend school for she is needed to care for him every day while the older women work.

The boy's enthusiastic grin and gurgling outbursts indicate his apparent joy from being rocked and cradled high above his customary hammock. I love his slobbering uncensored joy. He knows nothing of his physical restrictions, his label of poverty, nor is he burdened by fear. His whole being is an expression of masterful living.

1

Within the hut is a meticulous grouping of metal wash bins, cooking pots, and homemade brooms. The walls are embellished with soiled, dusty pictures torn from out-dated calendars and magazine advertisements most likely published in regions far away. In one photo, a bright smile decorates the face of a young woman drinking from a bottle of soda. In another, a powdered and flawless-faced Asian beauty seems overjoyed with some sort of cookie or cracker. An orchid rests behind her black, silky hair. The writing is indiscernible. The faces in these advertisements are remarkably disparate to the women who sleep, eat, and manage the lives of children, husbands, and relatives who call these walls home.

Here in the outskirts of Siem Reap, Cambodia, village women age far more rapidly than those in westernized environments. Years of physical labor coupled with malnutrition and multiple childbirths help ravage complexions, teeth, and immune systems.

It's a stark and primitive existence for those who have not made the leap from village to town.

Other children run giddily around the hut. All are partially clothed and their broad, infectious smiles lose none of their luster in spite of rotted teeth. Distended bellies cover the evidence of parasitic worms invading their intestines. Yet here they are, happy, laughing, and engaged in the universal game of peek-a-boo—showing off for the dozen visitors I have brought here this morning.

We are digging and installing a fresh water well—a method developed by years of trial and error excavation attempts involving augers, PVC piping, a generator, and a lot of native ingenuity and muscle. We are supervised by a local team of laborers who allow us Westerners to have a go at the digging and drilling. Once the water source is tapped, piping and pumps are installed followed by quality control checks for contaminants. When all is good, we are privileged to bear witness to a significant change in the infrastructure of this multi-generational family's life.

It has been nearly a decade since I first visited this area. After multiple failed attempts at establishing sustainable support, this well, now our one hundred twelfth, is due in part to collaborative efforts with other organizations—a testament to staying faithful to a vow.

In 2004, when first arriving in Cambodia, I played tour host to a group who joined me on one of my yearly Sacred Site excursions. The main attraction was the ancient wonder known as Angkor Wat, one of the oldest and largest spiritual temple complexes in the world. Dating back to the 12th century, these indescribable structures are a must for anyone who hungers to see the heights of what human creativity and ancient engineering can achieve. Carvings both vast and detailed tell the story of Hindu and Buddhist origins, bringing legendary history to life in ways language can never describe.

Yet as spectacular as these temples are, the greatest attraction, for me, is the Cambodian people themselves.

At the time of my first visit, little more than 30 years lay between my group walking the territory of the infamous Killing Fields and the genocide incited by the Cambodian Communist revolutionary Pol Pot, whose brutal ethnic cleansing mandates claimed the lives of millions. Only thirty years. Surprisingly, however, I encountered not one Cambodian harboring the slightest amount of bitterness or rage. There was an atmosphere of equanimity that seemed mismatched with the extreme poverty of third world environments where global wealth distribution and income equality leave places like Cambodia in their profitable dust.

Traveling the world has gifted me with a humbling perspective on how blessed I am. My level of material good is not even a concept in the minds of these villagers who somehow manage a life of survival and meaning. In fact, any of us in westernized cultures, regardless of what economic class we file ourselves under, are viewed as immeasurably affluent.

Thus the greatest gift that accompanies anyone willing to navigate his way across the planet is perspective—the brilliant offering given to one's consciousness with sacred delivery.

By removing ourselves from the take-for-granted myopic experience of western world amenities, we can awaken to a profound realization of how much we have and how often we forget such privilege.

Without perspective we become blind to our own blessings.

This self-sanctioned blindness breeds those who see only through a lens of comparison. The grass is always greener somewhere else—contentment is illusory and the hunter-gatherer instinct becomes driven by ego rather than by the natural desires for nourishment and conscious expansion.

Without some form of conscious realization, our longings become groomed by the imagery of advertisements, artificial conversation, faux news, and someone else's opinion. The belief in the necessity to compete for more becomes our mental infant that we must raise, nurture, and continuously feed, though its hunger is bottomless. We start coveting what our literal and metaphoric neighbor has and thus discount our own brand of being.

A general assertion, yes, but if we are honest, we would admit that we regularly compare ourselves to others. The ceiling of what we crave seems to be the floor upon which another treads. Our wanting to be something more from a current disdain of self, to have what someone else has, becomes a cycle of never enough that leads stereotypically to bitterness and contempt for others' successes.

And yet longing and desire, that innate hunger to explore and expand, is a propulsive instinct inside all of us. The baby desires to stand, the budding artist to express, the athlete to compete.

So is it the wanting, longing, or desire that creates a toxic disposition towards life or is it the bubble of unconsciousness that can envelop it?

The boy squirms more and it is clear from the stare of his devoted sister that it is time for me to give him back to her. With careful attention, I place him back into the arms he's most familiar with and step outside the hut. The sun blasts bright with dutiful precision.

Everyone in my group has gravitated to where they feel led. There is the well digging and the well-digging cheerleaders. There is a makeshift distribution center where others are passing out garden seeds of long-bean, lemongrass, cassava, and maize. And others play with the children, using plastic bottles as drum sticks and rocks as Legos to make imaginary temples and palaces in the heat-baked dirt.

Watching all of this from the front of the boy's hut, my perspective is once again restored to how ridiculously blessed my life is, just as it is every time I return to this country.

I recall sitting beneath a shade tree in front of the moat which runs along the front of the temple, Angkor Wat, several years into my commitment to serve here. I became fixated on an elderly woman, weathered face, head tied in rags, legs bent in squatting position as she stationed herself at the end of the stone portal entrance, a begging bowl resting at her feet.

For a moment our eyes met and I longed to know what she must think of all the tourists that pass her each day. I wondered what she might say to me had we the chance to share the same language.

"You, white man, imperial, living God-like. You have nothing to fear and everything to gain."

"Thank you. I get it," I answer to my own internal dialogue.

For her there is nothing else I need to achieve, nothing I need long for or strive to gain. I am Brahman. Nirvana is my home.

The grass (life) is green (abundant and fertile) right here.

Her assumed words become my truth.

In someone else's belief, you are rich and free.
In someone else's eyes you are smart, capable, and
daring.
In someone else's world of existence you have it all.
In someone else's level of experience you have already
reached their understanding of nirvana.
Whatever your story is, you are as blessed as you are
willing to recognize you are.

We *are* in nirvana. We are *already* in heaven. Yet in order for each of us to experience this, we must first recognize its existence.

In order to experience heaven on Earth, we must think, choose, and welcome its presence around us. We must recognize this divine energy even in the apparent absence of it. For by seeing it mentally, we draw it forth materially.

It is the law of cause and effect, a principle contained within every fiber of the cosmos.

I initiate a choice within my thought atmosphere about a desire—a "yes I can" or "no I can't" mental decision. This thought impresses itself upon my subjective atmosphere—the part of the mind that receives each thought, impartially, and begins magnetizing to me the very desire chosen.

I choose the thought "I live in a world of harmony," then by law, my world unfolds with harmonious patterning. I choose the thought "I live in a world filled with prejudice and strife," then my world is darkened with painful, unjust occurrences. Same world, different thoughts.

Cambodia teaches me to see how I walk upon a greener grass of possibility—a heaven on earth existence.

7

And, admittedly, that awareness took years of practice.

A decade before, I had no idea the dramatic turn my life would take after entering this country.

With my first tour group of fifteen, we landed in the humid, frenetically energized town of Siem Reap. It was immediately apparent that we had traveled to a plane of existence where the polarities of our human condition were transparently displayed.

There were the "haves"—those of us touring—and the "have nots"—the locals.

There seemed to be a watershed of filth and poverty in vast supply when venturing off the main road where palatial hotels for foreigners stood gleaming through the haze of the dust-filled air.

It was not long into our visit before everyone in the group repeatedly suggested we find a way to give back, someplace to assist. I approached our guide with a simple question, "Where in Siem Reap do you feel is the greatest need and how can we offer appropriate assistance?"

This young man looked at us and simply said, "Tonle Sap."

The Tonle Sap Lake is the largest mass of water in this part of Southeast Asia. In the dry season the banks recede dramatically and the caked mud becomes home for transients, gypsies, refugees—the poorest of the poor. Among the dwellers are innumerable malnourished children, many abandoned from families, some with limbs missing from the legacy of landmines that became synonymous with the Khmer Rouge destruction.

The guide shared how the Tonle Sap was where we would find the greatest density of hunger among children. Feeding them anything, something, became our mission.

Rallying the group, we purchased local foods to avoid any shock to sensitive digestive systems. We descended upon several local vendors and kept buying and buying, loading up two vans with bags and boxes of tamarind, banana, mango chunks, sticky rice treats, milk, bread, and more. We managed to buy all of the products from three side-by-side family vendors. When the purchases were totaled, it came to a whopping eighty-six US dollars.

Eighty-six dollars.

I stood there, staring at the dirt road beneath my feet and shook my head in disbelief. How could we obtain so much and have it cost so little?

The green grass of infinite possibility starts its awakening. Even among the filth, the dust, the poverty, the genesis of a new idea is hungering to spring forth.

Our guide explained how we cannot simply show up with food and not have some form of chaos erupt among the many who are hungry. He suggested waiting long enough for him to get a message to whatever matriarch there was of the Tonle Sap area before we arrived. This was before cell phones were so universally widespread. His method of delivering that communication still remains a mystery. Nevertheless, on arrival, there were nearly one hundred children organized in lines, sitting on the dried river bank, their arms outstretched, reaching, grabbing for the supplies we had brought. Each face was a mixture of elation and desperation. Several of the older ones made sure that the tamarind, bananas, milk, and bread were getting into the hands of the smaller children. The organization was short lived, however, as our makeshift distribution descended into a feverish grabbing war. Word had somehow spread about our endeavors and more children now raced towards us from off in the distance. In what felt like a sparse matter of minutes, it was done. The food supply was scattered among the many and the children began to slowly trickle off.

My auto-pilot energy, having kicked in to get the job done, suddenly waned and I felt a tremendous pressure expanding in my chest. Raw emotion swirled inside me. Vulnerable, messy. I looked around for someplace to retreat because nothing within my usual arsenal of coping skills seemed suitable to manage what wanted to be released. I crawled feverishly into a pontoon boat tied to a piling on the shore. I scrambled towards the rear and began sobbing with primal, guttural emotion. These were not tears of pity. This was different. Something physiological was happening inside me. Unprecedented. Enigmatic. My heart was literally breaking open. This experience, these children had somehow helped midwife the birth of a mystical and life-changing way of being. I felt them. I *was* them. And I knew that I could never return to my life with the same structure I had before.

It was there, crouched on my knees in that boat on the smelly, polluted Tonle Sap, that I made a vow to return, to do whatever was feasible in bringing yet-to-be solutions to the children here.

We do not have to travel across the world and be exposed to famine to have our hearts broken open. Our souls forever draw us to one continuous expansive op-portunity after another—opportunities to move beyond our present day limitations. Sometimes it simply takes the seeming extreme to finally get our attention. We take loved ones for granted only to feel deeply regretful upon their passing. We complain about our jobs only to become vulnerable when they end. We fail to appreciate our own bodies' ability to move, see, and hear until one or all of these senses are compromised.

The soul within beckons us to pay attention, to see that everything around us is fertile ground to have our hearts freed from petty restriction. Indeed, the grass is very, very green right beneath us, awaiting recognition.

It took that eighty-six dollar moment to launch the mo-tivation and thus the decision to know something greater was possible here. That I could do something, something sustainable if I became devoted to the possibility.

1) In what areas of your life have you futurized your good? For example, where have you told yourself that when a certain thing is over, then and only then will you be free to explore what makes you happy? When a certain obstacle is clear then and only then can you begin feeling the long desired relief that comes with solution? Consider how this form of thinking pushes those things further away from your ability to experience them.

2) What would it feel like to imagine having those desires fully in existence right now?

3) How could you incorporate a "grass is greener right now" mentality with the four main areas of your human journey?

The grass is greener right now in regards to my health. I am willing to experience that by doing _____.

The grass is greener right now in regards to my financial status. I am willing to experience that by doing _____.

The grass is greener right now in regards to my career and creative expression. I am willing to experience that by doing _____.

The grass is greener right now in regards to my love relationships. I am willing to experience that by doing _____.

Beginner's Allowing

> He might have been naive, but he didn't care; he
> said he'd rather die with his heart on his sleeve than
> end up another cynic.
>
> — Colum McCann, *Let the Great World Spin*

In 1978, after my freshman year in college, I toured in a
summer music group for Oral Roberts University. My willing
participation became entangled with feelings of hypocrisy.

Attending Oral Roberts in Tulsa, Oklahoma was not my
first or desired choice. I had long wanted to explore a career
in journalism, and the fiery thrill of receiving a scholarship
to North Texas State for their undergraduate program was
reduced to smoldering ash by my mother's religious extin-
guisher. She downplayed the acceptance letter I proudly
showed her with a simple, "The Lord told me . . ."

When your mother begins a sentence with "The Lord
told me . . ." there is little or no room for argument.

How can one successfully gain any traction to an
emotional appeal with such an auspicious, authoritative
debater?

13

"The Lord told me that you are to go to Oral Roberts University," she stated emphatically.

She had watched her fair share of weekly telecasts and envisioned me there among the highly glossed, shellac-covered young adults, dutifully singing and being educated in a Christian environment far more suited to our Assemblies of God upbringing.

It became fruitless to debate the matter and eventually I caved in, applied, and was accepted there.

After my father's death some eleven years prior, my mother had received a small social security benefit for myself and my siblings while we were still minors. My portion would start coming directly to me in order to help pay for books. And now that she had remarried, Mom planned to enroll my stepdad in helping to cover some of the tuition expenses. I'd work odd jobs. I'd search for additional scholarship monies. I'd take it a semester at a time.

Fulfilling her expectations also clashed with the reality that I simply did not want to be there. I had long since grown weary of the religious dogma that had saturated my entire existence. That journalism scholarship was my ticket out. Now that ticket had been traded in for a less desirable excursion.

One afternoon, while passing through the Activities building during winter midterm exams of my freshman year, I saw a posted announcement on the student activity board.

Auditions – Summer Music Ministries Program
Full Summer Commitment
Tuition Scholarship Monies Awarded

14

Here it was, an opportunity to reduce my mounting tuition.

I learned that the primary mission of these music groups or "tour bands" was to travel the country during summer break, promoting the University and persuading youth to consider ORU as a viable educational option.

Thus my hypocrisy. The possibility of getting tuition support won out over any remorse I might collect from proselytizing and luring those who may have been more successful at resisting their mother's visions.

In spite of being a mere freshman and competing against scores of upper classmates, I managed to get accepted, placed into one of several tour bands, and began frequent rehearsals, religious tutelage, and etiquette instruction on how not to be a slob in a host's home. It was a summer filled with innumerable concerts and innumerable casseroles, driving from one scheduled church stop to the next. Long hours became long days as my band mates and I crammed inside a mini tour bus, covering the Southern region states we had been assigned. We sang about the glories of God, Oral Roberts, and actively recruited for that space-aged looking university.

I was miserable and hot. Even so, I learned how to eat around gnats when given a cucumber and mayonnaise sandwich outdoors during an Arkansas summer church social.

Jerry Florence, who later became one of my singing partners in the 80's trio Alliance, was in charge of these ORU music groups. He was a new graduate, working for the

University by running this particular outreach program—overseeing tour schedules, bookings, and accommodations.

Jerry and I bonded that summer when he would make surprise "spot checks" on each band's performances. At 19, I lacked male role models and I soon became enamored by Jerry's musical talents and business savvy. He paid attention to me. He challenged my vocal performances and offered guidance. With this connection, I thought, maybe the voice my mother had heard the year before was indeed accurate. I was becoming more and more accepting of this educational choice and willing to see how this environment might be okay after all. Yet partway into our summer touring, Jerry learned that the University would not be renewing his contract. They were cutting the program and he would not be coming back to the Tulsa, Oklahoma campus in the fall.

Disappointments surface when we fail to adopt wider parameters for what we expect will bring us contentment. I expected my scholarship to be my path to freedom. I expected this newly established relationship with Jerry to pacify my discontent with college and make it all better. At 19, I didn't know any better than to rely on outside things to dictate my fulfillment.

When people or events become our *all or nothing*, there will undoubtedly be unfulfilled expectations. People make mistakes. People leave. Opportunities seem to wither and die and we experience the sadness, disappointment, and fear that apparent limitation and loss bring along. Events, conditions, weather, trends—everything fluctuates and changes. If we haven't learned to be content with the present moment, regardless of the effects before us, then our relationship with expectation becomes soured and negative.

Thus the big question: How do we maintain healthy expectations even with a history of disappointment?

Like any awareness and desire for change, we start where we are.

Seeing where we might hold within us an all-or-nothing sensibility, we begin a journey of willingness to explore something less rigid by starting with the following.

Accept Wider Parameters

Creating a multitude of choices and practicing non-attachment to any of them dramatically reduces disappointment. You can still expect to have a fulfilling experience but you are flexible to when and how it will unfold.

Letting go of the "how" is one of the greatest gifts we can give ourselves. Too often we lock into an idea that our good must come from this job, our love must come from this person, our approval must come from this group, community, or teacher(s). Not only is this a recipe for assured disappointment, it also projects upon them a responsibility that was never theirs to begin with. Our good—whether love, encouragement, money, success, you name it—is already out there. It is already a living, breathing, viable energy. If we don't open up to greater parameters of meeting and greeting it, then we have no right to project blame upon another.

17

Value the Lessons

Being able to value the lessons that come with change is vital. If you consider that everything that crosses your field of experience can either build you up or break you down, then the practice of expanding your consciousness must be precipitated by willing flexibility.

My earliest mentor, Louise Hay, implored me to remember one thing above all else. "Honor the entirety of your journey." Every stumble, every heartbreak, every misstep is vital fuel in moving us forward with a refinement and discernment that only comes from experience. Each mark on the timeline of our lives is a link in a chain that got us to where we are today. Learn to value each link rather than wishing it were not so.

Return to Your Innocence

Begin to approach everything you do with a beginner's mind. No history, no false need to protect or shield. Just make a daily decision to live life as if what you ultimately seek is also seeking you. It is being the beginner with untarnished expectation.

I once heard a teacher remark that the four most dangerous words ever spoken are, "I know that already."

Jerry talked of doing something *wild and crazy* the week after the tour ended and before my school year resumed. He asked if I wanted to go along and stake out some kind of adventure and I responded as any hero-worshiping teen would do to his newest idol. I screamed, "Yes!"

18

He came up with the idea of deep sea fishing in Aransas Pass, a port somewhere off Padre Island in South Texas. It wasn't a particularly "wild" choice but neither of us had ever been and it sounded like one of those rugged items you'd have on your list of *100 things to do before you die*.

We took Dramamine for 24 hours prior to our departure and yet, as we bounded out to sea, I still felt as though everything I had ever eaten might revisit me. Traveling miles and miles in the predawn darkness, the boat rocked and hurled from side to side on the choppy waters of the Gulf of Mexico. I breathed deeply and bargained with the equilibrium gods to intervene.

After sunrise, I was able to get a closer inspection of our fellow journeymen. Jerry and I were the only ones on the boat who were not fishermen by trade. We were surrounded by seasoned pros wearing equally seasoned, salt-stained caps and carrying extra lures in their moist pockets.

Jerry had gotten us onto a commercial charter. Not a tourist charter. Not an "oh, let's just cast a line out and enjoy the day" charter. No, this was where each man looked at the other with a sense of distrust, wanting to taint the others' bait buckets with some homemade, concocted fish repellant. This was competitive fishing. This was ESPN fishing. This was the *crazy* part of the *wild and crazy*.

I decided to pretend I knew what I was doing. I baited and cast my line.

No sooner had I settled in for some ripple watching when I got a hard jolt on the end of my rod. The reel began to spin. It dispensed the fishing line so fast that I froze while the nylon cord emptied out into the choppy water.

"*Nothing* happens on the first cast," I remember hearing from the others. Then the shouting of the men on board snapped me out of my daze and I began pulling back and bucking the line, gripping harder on the handle, and watching the pole arch and bend as I strained to hold on. My knuckles were white from lack of blood flow and the mystery on the other end seemed hell-bent on rebelling. Grunting and gasping out, "scuse me," I started crawling over and under the rest of the fishermen that encircled the deck. Round and round I went, and every time I got to starboard, they all shouted Three! then Four! Five! Six! *Six* times around the boat as the yet-to-be-seen fish dragged me in circles.

On that sixth round, several sympathizers gathered around me with a net and a bunch of extra hands to help raise my catch out of the water.

There it was, at last—a 47-pound King Mackerel.

The weigh station attendant on shore commented that it was one of the largest caught in those waters all summer.

Several men high-fived me with "Congratulations," but the majority of them simply gave me the hard stare, muttering under their breaths, "Beginner's luck."

Beginner's luck . . .

As a practicing metaphysician, I've learned to let go of the notion of luck. There is no randomness involved in creation. Creation is deliberate. Everything unfolds for us in accordance to our consciousness. As above, so below. So it stands to reason that this anomaly seen as *beginner's luck* may be more accurately defined as *beginner's allowing*.

As beginners in anything, we haven't yet developed our muscles of cynicism. We're not clinging to our disappointment or the resistance accompanied with doubt. With beginners, there's still a sense of optimism—a childlike clean slate of acceptance where all kinds of possibilities stand on tiptoe. A natural expectancy of good that seems to whisper to us *of course*. *Of course* you caught the fish. *Of course* you got the job. *Of course* you made a perfect score on your exam. When being *on course*, we live unencumbered, not jaded by the perspective that sometimes accompanies those who've been around life's block. As beginners we're in a much greater state of natural allowing. Consciousness responds to that, creating demonstration the way it always can be—swift and natural.

When we look at our relationship to what we expect, so many of us plant seeds of futility, disappointment, and judgment based on our collective history.

Are you willing to look at how your history has served you rather than crippling your present and your yet-to-be future? I managed, some would say even thrived, through those final years at ORU. In fact, I proved to myself that I could attend a full class load and work and maintain a decent GPA—something that set me up well when arriving unseasoned and naïve for my first year as a wannabe actor pounding the pavement in New York City.

Those first months in the Big Apple paralleled my experience on that boat. I didn't know that I wasn't supposed to do certain things. I didn't know that you couldn't simply walk into casting agencies and ask to speak to a theatrical agent. By not knowing the rules, I wasn't bound by the rules and I found, more often than not, that there was a waiting and willing exchange, a helping hand, even a job due to what some considered brazen behavior. It wasn't brazen. It was beautiful, unpolluted naiveté.

I didn't know that you had to work years at getting into the acting unions, do your time, struggle, manipulate, and beg. I would buy the trade papers every week, read through all the auditions carefully, and map out my temporary office job schedule to accommodate the auditions. One week I saw an audition for a tour production for the musical Grease, but instead of the casting call being held in New York City, they were seeing union actors only in Philadelphia. I was neither union nor did I have any idea how to get to Philadelphia.

I had just reconnected with a college friend who had chosen the path of priesthood. He invited me to his seminary deep in the borough of Queens. He took me around the quarters, introducing me to the other seminarians and deacons who were living on the premises. Over a meal with these clergymen, I happened to mention the Philadelphia audition. Before I could even muster an objection, they passed a hat, reached into their wallets, threw in cash, and told me to buy a train ticket and take my chances on being seen.

I took the train to Philadelphia and got the job. I received my Actors Equity union card barely six months into my Manhattan residency.

Author Nils Sköld wrote in his book *Experience Slows You Down*, "What an industry needs is people who have no idea on how it operates, people that don't know that there are any rules. While it is good to break rules and to push boundaries, it's much better to just never know that any rules exist. So when an agency boasts that they have years of experience in the field that your company is working in, run the other way, 'cause that only means that they know the rules. You need someone who doesn't."

Go back to the beginning. *Allow* greater parameters, more options, flexibility. Allow without the attachment of futile conditions. Allow with the zeal of a child at Christmas. Allow because you understand that nothing is separating you from your good but your directed thought.

That state of purity still exists within each of us. It waits for recognition. Are you willing to recognize it and welcome it into your immediate experience? Doing so does not require you to have the "how" figured out. In fact the "how" is really none of your business. The simple requirement of returning to beginner's allowing is letting go of the need to control and opening the door of your life to that steadfast creative energy.

Strengthen your allowing by beginning to simply breathe in, saying to yourself, *"I Allow."* On the exhale say, *"I Release All Resistance."*

Inhale "I Allow."

Exhale "I Release All Resistance."

I go for weeks at a time using this simple breathing mantra as my entire meditation. My aim? To become more and more a vessel for conscious *allowing*, more and more to look at the "big catches" in life and naturally say, *"Of course."*

1) Can you recall a time when your green-behind-the-ears' innocence actually worked in your favor?

2) In what present situations can you begin the practice of accepting wider parameters?

3) "Don't lose the lesson" is often shared as a reminder not to waste time in regret. Looking back, what mistakes gave rise to some of your most profound insights? If you could, would you go back and change the circumstances? If so, why?

4) What are you ready to allow more of? Are you willing to release all resistance, all excuses to that which you long for?

Cupcakes

> Gratitude turns what we have into enough, and more. It turns denial into acceptance, chaos into order, confusion into clarity . . . it makes sense of our past, brings peace for today, and creates a vision for tomorrow.
>
> – Melody Beattie

740 CAPACITY read the sign in bold black letters on the gymnasium wall, yet by 1987 more than 800 people were showing up. The weekly Wednesday meeting had grown so swiftly over the past few years that the venue had moved several times and there simply weren't enough seats for the scores of people pouring through the door. The fire marshal had become a weekly visitor.

From all over the United States, Mexico, Canada, Great Britain, and beyond, those seeking comfort and answers flocked to this two-hour-plus meeting hoping to find some sanity in it all.

Everyone at the meeting in West Hollywood Park in Los Angeles had come to see and seek solace from author and metaphysician Louise Hay. This weekly gathering, called the Hay Ride, an affectionate title attributed to its leader, was heralded as the first spiritual support group of its kind formulated to meet the needs of those challenged by AIDS. The meeting got its start a few years prior with a pleading phone call from a diagnosed man. Louise invited him and a few of his friends to sit in her living room to explore ways to comfort one another in the emotionally paralyzing beginnings of the epidemic. By the next week the group had tripled in size and, like the disease that prompted it all, the meeting never stopped growing.

Many people contend it was the disease that made Louise Hay the titan that changed the spiritual landscape of America and subsequently advanced her brand worldwide. In a 2008 interview, New York Times writer Mark Oppenheimer suggests, "Without the AIDS epidemic, Louise Hay would be another workshop leader taking predominantly middle-class white women on retreats where they recite affirmations, short statements meant to bring a new, desired reality to fruition."

Regardless of public opinion or projection, she was a compassionate voice to the modern day outcast, the ones stigmatized with a leprosy-like immune ravaging disease, the likes of which our modern society had not seen before. Her presence was not a strategy for fame. It was simply comme il faut for anyone who operated with an open heart.

AIDS was and continues to be no respecter of persons. In that uncharacteristic gymnasium, it brought together the young and old, professionals and poor, all sitting side by side, raw with emotion, looking to Louise for guidance or tools—most praying she would tell them everything was going to be okay.

It was a tricky place to open your heart. It was not uncommon to befriend and grow close to the many who found the courage to share their challenges and their resources to this group, only to lose them weeks later to the disease. Yet faithfully and vulnerable the diagnosed came, many having to replace their well-worn and comfortable community of friends and colleagues with those who would now embrace them with understanding rather than rejecting them with warped judgments regarding their morality.

Parents, many discovering that a child was gay AND ill all in one avalanche of emotion, wandered in with glazed eyes. Women, minorities, clergy, and large legions of empathic supporters gathered week after week, sharing their struggles, their hopes, everyone silently pleading to their respective God for a cure.

My friends Jerry Florence, Keith Kimberlin, and I not only ran the sound equipment for these gatherings but also began composing and singing songs that reinforced Louise's message of self-love and nurturing. We opened and closed every gathering by chanting "Doors opening. Doors closing. I am safe. It's only change," and offering up Louise's theme song, "I love myself the way I am."

One memorable night after the chanting, a mother stood up to share.

Like so many mothers before her, she glanced over the crowd, her watery eyes adjusting to the hundreds of faces staring back at her. She hesitated, creating a huge lingering

27

inhale, as if breathing in a dose of oxygenated courage, and then began.

"We have a little ritual in our family," she started.

"Many years ago—gosh, I can't even tell you when now—my son Timothy suggested that we celebrate everything. He had read or seen something about an orphanage in Africa or Asia—I really can't remember the specifics—but it spoke about the resilience of these children. Even in the midst of famine, war, disease, these children had formed a bond without adult supervision or coaching. They had adapted an untainted affinity for supporting the well-being of each other. They watched out for the welfare of their peers, praised one another, and shared their authentic joy when one mastered academic success or found a foster home. I guess somehow they knew this would make their journey seem less alone and that together they would somehow create a better life. They shared their whole being with each other and seemed to find a way to celebrate everything.

"One day my son announced that, as a family, we were going to do the same. We laughed. But he was determined that we were going to 'have an experience' like those children.

"What are you going to do with that but humor him? Timothy's persistence could be bottled and sold.

"So it started out as a simple bonding practice but it grew into something far deeper and more meaningful than any of us imagined. Over time, we started to experiment with what it meant to celebrate everything. When I say everything, I mean *everything*. Whether it was a glowing report card from one of my kids or a traffic ticket, we celebrated.

28

Whether it was getting a new puppy or my husband being laid off, we celebrated. The goal was to do our best at not judging events in our lives as good or bad but to just view them as part of life's curriculum. Learn from them, uncover the lessons, and do our best to grow—to celebrate it all. Less than a year into the ritual, we started making cupcakes. Every week we would stand at our kitchen counter, raise one of the freshly baked cupcakes in the air, and make a celebratory toast at whatever event life had brought us.

"Quite honestly, when I developed breast cancer, it was challenging for me to stand at that counter, hold up that cupcake, and feel that there was anything about this situation that I could celebrate. Yet we had agreed—no matter what.

"So week after week, with my hair falling out, nauseated from chemo, I stood with my kids and my husband and celebrated life as best I could. My daughter even decorated the tops with icing stick figures that depicted long flowing hair to make me feel better about my looks. Something about that unfailing ritual kept pivoting my focus towards the good and I attribute being cancer-free for over five years now to the steadfastness of standing at that counter with my family and celebrating.

"Timothy moved here to Los Angeles, my daughter off to college in the Midwest. But we managed with the tradition long-distance, over the phone. Sometimes I'd make cupcake care packages and send them. It was a way to stay involved in each other's lives as best as possible."

She hesitated. Her gaze drifted towards the floor, then she continued.

29

"Today's cupcake has been the hardest to swallow," she said shakily, her voice filling with emotion.

"My son Timothy died last night from his many challenges with AIDS. Pneumonia set in and for the last week he has needed assistance in breathing. He kept slipping in and out of consciousness. I purchased a cupcake every morning at the grocery near my hotel and brought it with me to the hospital. I would place it on the tray in front of him. Sometimes I placed it on his chest. It brought me comfort to watch the cupcake rise and fall with his breath. It told me there was still life in his body, there was still a chance that my baby would live.

"When it was obviously too much for him, he simply gave up and let go.

"I'm so, so angry," she said shakily, her watery gaze now rising to readdress the crowd.

"I'm angry that my baby boy is gone. I'm angry that the world will never get to experience the heart of this young man and the good that always seemed to follow wherever he went."

She breathed in a long, deliberate, dauntless breath and her trembling words were now accompanied by a steady flow of tears.

"And," she paused, breathing harder, "I know how much Timothy would hate this. He would not want me to stay like this. Otherwise, what would be the point of his life? What would be his legacy?"

And with that she reached in her coat pocket and brought out something wrapped in tin foil. She peeled away the folded layers to reveal a cupcake.

"My family stood around our hotel coffee table this morning—my daughter, husband, and I—and I tried, I really tried to toast Timothy but I just couldn't. I had to get out of there. I had to scream at something. I stood on the curb of our hotel intersection and just yelled at the traffic. I yelled at the sky, at God. It all felt so deeply unfair."

She recounted how the entire day had been reduced to a blur of tearful release.

And with a profound plea for help, she ended her story. "So I was wondering if tonight you would be like those orphaned village children and help me out?"

In the raw beauty of that unforgettable moment, she lifted the cupcake in the air.

The rest of us, following, lifted a symbolic cupcake in the air to make a toast.

"To Timothy," she reverently spoke, "in celebration of a life well-lived. May I never forget your example. May I always see the vision of something greater. May I continue to celebrate and honor it all."

Moments such as these—moments that teach us what is precious and what is real—moments that remind us that in and through all things, whether we can see it or not, there is unfailing beauty and grace—that is the true essence of living. When we focus on anything other than that constant divinity, we deny life.

It was a night that changed the trajectory of my life. I could not get the premise of expressing gratitude for everything out of my mind. I noticed how often my petty experiences were heightened and prolonged by complaint. I noticed how my own battles with my heart and the following years of misdiagnosis, mystery, and debilitation would ultimately lead me to view it all through the lens of that mother's story.

How would the quality of our lives change if we were to stand around the counters of our collective kitchens and, without fail, celebrate each day? Could we develop the willingness to seek out the divine order that is operating in the nonphysical as well as the physical and begin allowing ourselves to experience the majesty of this world with pure intent?

The poet Mary Oliver wrote, "When it's over, I want to say: all my life I was a bride married to amazement. I was the bridegroom, taking the world into my arms. When it is over, I don't want to wonder if I have made of my life something particular, and real. I don't want to find myself sighing and frightened, or full of argument. I don't want to end up simply having visited this world."

Given that our time in this physical body is temporary, then it stands that taking the world into our arms is a decision that must be practiced through gratitude.

Wherever we go, if we are willing to pay attention, there are collectives of individuals living like those children in the orphanage, demonstrating what bonding, support, and authentic gratitude look like. It is displayed through the actions of people, depicted in stories we read, embedded in the lyrics of music, and lived out by cultures and people who have measurably greater excuses to give in to bitterness and futility than we ever will.

I believe the Timothys of the world teach us an elevated way to live. The more we honor their example and carry on the tradition of gratitude, the more our years here are optimized and the legacies we leave endure.

May we all raise a cupcake in the air and salute the good as it weaves its beauty in and through each precious day.

1) How important is the practice of gratitude in your life? In what ways do you incorporate it consciously into your day-to-day activity?

2) I had never seen that mother before nor did I ever see her again after that profound night. Yet her story changed my life. What moments, encounters, experiences have happened to you that altered the trajectory of your own path?

3) What beginning steps would endear you to a life of "amazement" as the poet Mary Oliver writes?

Beautifully Broken

> It is the height of arrogance to prescribe a moral code or health regime or spiritual practice as an amulet to keep things from falling apart. Things do fall apart. It is in their nature to do so. When we try to protect ourselves from the inevitability of change, we are not listening to the soul. We are listening to our fear of life and death, our lack of faith, our smaller ego's will to prevail. To listen to your soul is to stop fighting with life—to stop fighting when things fall apart; when they don't go our way, when we get sick, when we are betrayed or mistreated or misunderstood. To listen to the soul is to slow down, to feel deeply, to see ourselves clearly, to surrender to discomfort and uncertainty and to wait.
>
> – Elizabeth Lesser

Day after day, the artisan would fill the molds and start the assembly line process of creating his signature clay pots. One after the other, these pots, made from the local clay that lined the banks of the town's river, emerged from his kiln, each identical in shape and detail. Once fully dried, he prepared them for sale at market. There was only one significant problem. Hardly anyone was buying. Despite his best efforts, sales never rose above the meager mark. Believing in a "more is better" approach, he worked longer and harder to create a bigger inventory, yet nothing was changing. The pots continued to sit unclaimed or even bargained for month after unprofitable month. Finally, with so many of the unsold pots vying for space, he began running out of room within the shop to store them. Every inch of the floor lay cluttered except for a single haphazard aisle barely wide enough for his frail, thin frame to maneuver. Towering stacks like clay stalagmites rose from the floors, eventually blocking out the sun that longed to peek through each day from the storefront window.

One morning, while making his way through a narrow opening, the artisan caught his foot on the edge of one of the stacked columns of pots. It leaned, wobbled, and fell, hitting one row after another across the huddled floor. Broken fragments of clay scattered all around his feet.

He screamed, his voice tapping deep into the chambers of frustration and helplessness he had long, long repressed. Bending down, his defeated hands touched each piece as if to apologize for failing to find them a home. He placed the remains in the burlap bags used to transport the pots to market. "These bags aren't going to market," he thought dejectedly. "They are bound for the trash."

It was hard to think of simply throwing the gathered bits away. He had, after all, dug the clay himself from the banks of the river. He had meticulously separated and removed each pebble and fragment of tree root and brush grass before the clay went into the mold.

Staring at the collection of burlap bags that lay around him, the artisan began to cry. It had been a long while since he had shed an actual tear. So much of his current life was spent doing, thinking, planning that he'd pushed away his sadness, covering it up with the mindless work, the familiar task of making pots. But his sadness had never left and now it pressed at his weary heart with an undeniable need for attention. His crying continued, slowly then forcefully, until eventually, the last drop of emotion that would not be denied rolled downward from his swollen eyes.

It was then that the artisan began feeling a strange sensation. He discovered an ability to breathe easier, fuller, more calmly. It was as if releasing his long-held tears had opened up more space within him and allowed unclaimed air to fill his lungs.

While picking up the fragments around him, he spotted an old can of glue and some tubes of gold filigree long hidden behind the multitude of piles.

Suddenly the fresh air in his lungs was accompanied by a fresh idea.

He began gluing pieces back into formation, adding the gold in between the haphazard cracks. The result was so startlingly beautiful that the artisan further expanded his experiment by adding color from old paint stock he had forgotten existed in his inventory of supplies.

He set them outside his front door to dry.

The positive reaction was immediate.

Before the pots could even be transported to market, people began knocking on his shop door and asking to buy them with great enthusiasm and zeal.

"How unique, how beautiful," the passersby exclaimed as they left with multiple purchases and promises to tell their friends.

Today, the artisan continues pouring the clay in the mold just as before, but as soon as the kiln has fired them to perfection, he places the pots one by one in a burlap bag and purposefully breaks them, thus beginning his innovative and joyous process of gluing each unique piece back together.

Most of us have approached life like the artisan in the story. We get stuck in patterns, habits of doing, and fail to see other options until our patterns come crashing down. We go about seeking love and giving love based on our observations of others. We make considerations about our career paths by what family and faculty recommend or by what statistics dictate is the next sure thing. This gathering of data, this safe, cookie-cutter approach to making decisions is supposed to make us feel safe and comforted and hopefully keep us away from the pitfalls of life.

Yet it is our missteps, our heartbreaks (or heart expansions as I like to call them), the collective disappointments and stumbles followed by our recoveries that bring about the uncovering of our character.

Greg Baer, author of the book *Real Love*, says that true, unconditional love is "caring about the happiness of another person without any thought for what we might get for ourselves." That and that alone is real love. Not "if I do this, if I say this, if I give this, what will you give me in return?"

Real love has no agenda.

Turning that real love inward proves even more powerful.

Long ago, my friend Jeff mentioned to me a new spiritual practice he had started as part of a new year's resolution.

"I decided if I was going to explore self-love in a more expansive, radical way," said Jeff, "then I was determined to stand in front of a full length mirror naked and consciously send appreciative thoughts towards what I saw. For months, I kept at it and the practice was anything but easy. The first thing my focus went to was all of my perceived flaws. Yet, with each passing day, it became increasingly easier—a simple appreciation for the genius of the human body was unfolding before my very eyes. For instance, after a while, I didn't just see my hands. What I saw was an instrument of genius that could hold, move, build, create practically anything it was allowed to touch. Mine were not simply legs, but cosmic inventions that could carry me across the world if I propelled them to. Everything became more than just a body part—each part of me was a divine design given to me to use. In the beginning, this practice seemed far too simplistic and perhaps a waste of time, but it has helped propel my heart, my mind, my attitude to a deeper, authentic appreciation and value for who I am and how I should treat this instrument I've been given."

I was captivated by his enthusiasm and thought I'd try it myself. I had been in a cycle of physical neglect, letting my work schedule and a recent cross-country move become the excuse for not taking better care of myself. Like Jeff, all I could see at first was what I didn't like about myself. Like the artisan and the pieces of broken clay pots, I simply wanted to hide everything in an imaginary burlap bag. To add to the experience, I developed severe chest pains a week into the spiritual practice and eventually drove myself to the emergency room. My heart had gone into atrial fibrillation and the pain was accompanied by the doctor's discovery of a septic gallbladder. I underwent surgery, a stint in ICU, and a frustrating recovery. After finally returning home, I stood in front of my bathroom mirror recalling how I had begun this exercise weeks before.

I approached it once again, only now there were tremendous additions under the "flawed" column of my mental descriptive page. With surgical scars, bloating, and a shaved chest hair pattern that resembled something like a spastic crop circle, I made attempts to send appreciation and love to what I saw.

It was a sobering and difficult challenge. There were mornings of tremendous sadness and depression and the turnaround from pity to acceptance was a long, vulnerable process. Yet something kept drawing me back to try. Even in the midst of all this harshness, something was wanting to crack open. Buried resentments and wounds were finally being let out of some suppressed locked cage. Motivation for a real, substantial change, not just wishing for change, was returning and the initial practice, to simply appreciate what was before me, was finally given a sustainable amount of dedicated time. With each golden thought I took whatever misguided criticisms and broken feelings I had manufactured and began to slowly piece together a new view of myself. My recovery time was shortened. I was back on track and uncovering the best of me.

That was many years ago. And I have returned to that spiritual practice innumerable times. Is it because the times before didn't "take"? No, I believe, as in any relationship, we are continuously courting ourselves. There isn't just one date, one nice moment of recognition. It is a constant dance of paying respects, self-honoring and searching for greater ways of fulfilling that for ourselves. I feel I am continuously offered the chance to court myself back to wholeness—a potential way of being that is far beyond anything I may ever be capable of measuring.

Broken to Broken Open

As a full-time New Thought minister with a diverse membership, I have determined the following adage to be true: people show up for our services from two motivations—one is inspiration and the other is desperation. The desperate motivation, for the most part, is not always obvious in the way people present themselves. Yet, over time, if there is frequent attendance and the beginnings of any sort of community participation, facades begin to dissolve and I get a sense of the theme of thought that surrounds them. So often that theme has to do with their history of religious wounding and the burdensome baggage carried from an incessant "wretch like me" repetitive message still vocal and vibrant within their subjective belief systems.

The philosophy of New Thought and all its brother and sister organizations—Religious Science, Unity, Divine Science and other similar teachings—share a consistent message that you are enough as you are. You are loved by God, Source, the Divine Creator simply for who you are, not for what you might become.

In this message of inclusive acceptance, there comes a point when people learn that by dissolving all sense of blame of others and acknowledging responsibility for the quality of their lives, by virtue of their own thoughts, they can change their lives. It is powerful when a person can see this as liberating rather than diminishing, to know that by changing one's thinking, one can begin to change from a culture of surviving to thriving. This conscious choosing of thought offers freedom from life as victim, life as less than, life as unfair. Mind is creative and it is the medium by which we deliberately mold our relationship with the world through the conscious use of spiritual law. Yet if the theme of brokenness is too hardwired, then this becomes the moment when any thin-layered, warm and fuzzy, temporary comfort evaporates and those too attached to a wound, too immersed in a strong need to blame something outside themselves will make their exit. It is a compassionate yet sad observation. It can be challenging to cut the cord of blame when one is engulfed in a world so readily casting aspersions on every seeming level.

Brokenness, however, is not a destination. It is the inevitable enveloping energy that slaps at the face and pounds at the gut to remind us we are vessels of feeling. But what do we do with these feelings, with this seeming irreparable mess? Do we barricade ourselves from their raw presence or do we learn to breathe with them and through them, all the while learning that by allowing them the space to flow through us, we go from someone who is broken to someone who is broken open?

Author Vance Havner so eloquently stated, "God uses broken things. It takes broken soil to produce a crop, broken clouds to give rain, broken grain to give bread, broken bread to give strength. It is the broken alabaster box that gives forth perfume."

Being broken open revives us. It creates within us a spaciousness that did not exist before. The poet Rumi said, "The wound is the place where Light enters you." Our brokenness is the place where this leading light can penetrate through us and shine itself upon all the strengths, talents, and possibilities we had forgotten were in us.

Each of us will move towards being broken open when we are ready and not a moment or pleading conversation sooner. To me, that becomes one of the hardest lessons of our humanity—watching others remain in pain either by choice or ignorance.

Our "holy instant," as A Course in Miracles describes, is a moment of recognition, a moment of suspended judgment. To move away from our brokenness one suspended judgment at a time feels doable to even the most resistant.

In those moments, standing naked with our brokenness, can we be willing to accept that something greater exists for us?

Let us commit ourselves to a prayer of recognition. Let us repeatedly say with no reservations,

- I take responsibility for what I see.

- I willingly choose my thoughts and decide the quality of my life from this day forward.

- Everything that shows up in my life is exactly what I need to move me to my next level of greatness.

- I ask for the light of love to break open my heart and reveal to me the majestic nature of God.

- What I ask for, I receive. And I am grateful. Amen, and so it is.

1) The word "kintsukuroi" is a Japanese word which means "to repair with gold," the art of repairing pottery with gold or silver lacquer and understanding that the piece is more beautiful for having been broken. How can the art of "kintsukuroi" apply to you in the realms of emotional, physical, and spiritual "repair"?

2) What about the artisan and his habits might you relate to?

3) Broken hearts, setbacks, shattered dreams do not have to be concretized in tragedy. They can be the very catalysts into life's deepest satisfaction. Are there parts of your past that you have defined as irreparable? Are they, or have they just been left abandoned and await a fresh perspective?

4) What is the value of finding the beauty in our perceived imperfections?

5) Would you be willing to embark upon the mirror exercise? The goal is consistency. After one week, what changes in perception have you experienced about yourself? After two weeks, three, one month?

And We Are All Merely Players

Every Christmas season I find myself reflecting on my brother Doug and how he took his own life. Due to his predominant Major League Baseball status, his death made headlines within the sports world and lasting scars for those he left behind. Compelled to process our relationship through writing, I published the following piece several months after his death.

Doug Ault, 1950–2004

> All the world's a stage,
> And all the men and women merely players.
> They have their exits and their entrances,
> And one man in his time plays many parts.
>
> – Shakespeare

Life will always contain drama. Just as darkness shares the experience with light, so we share our years of conscious evolution with circumstances that contain challenges. This life has taught me that I have the opportunity to let my free will direct dramas that hopefully contain deep, life-altering meaning rather than vacuous soap operas. This particular drama involves two brothers—players as different in temperament and personality as in age.

My brother Doug was an anomalous creature. Ten years older than I, he seemed to have entered the world swinging. The constructive swinging came in the form of a baseball bat as he channeled that energy all the way to the major leagues. The destructive swinging came in the form of fists and fits of rage that were as unpredictable as the hurricanes that sometimes visited our little corner of the world in Texas. As a child, I learned to stay out of his way. Having once unknowingly provoked him, I found myself hurling through the air towards a wall where, on impact, I nearly bit my tongue in two.

Doug left home right after his high school graduation, pursuing dreams of playing baseball through various college scholarships, eventually landing a spot in the majors. He was as charismatic as he was volatile, and at 6' 4" tall, he was a handsome, giant presence that seemed to endear himself to sports fans as a destined iconic hero. He had managed to rise above the poverty of our upbringing and fashion himself into a seemingly successful sports figure. He broke records during his years with the Toronto Blue Jays, graced the pages of Sports Illustrated, and endorsed Brut Cologne for the folks in Canada.

My life path, my world, was vastly different and there was little to no interaction with him through the rest of my adolescence and early adulthood. It was rare that my family ever found themselves fully together. Usually, Doug was the one who never made it back. If he wasn't playing ball in the States, then he sought out ball-playing opportunities in other countries. He had married, had a child, divorced, had other relationships, had another child, remarried again.

In the ensuing years, the skills with which he had played baseball waned and he fought for and occasionally won various coaching positions with Triple A franchise teams. He also fought years of substance addictions exacerbated by on-the-job injuries.

It was never really discussed openly, but at some point my family knew that the absences were no longer about his work, but more about his lack of work and the dark descent one travels when you have robbed Peter so many times that Paul doesn't even expect payment anymore. His career had dried up and so had the inflated income he had relied on to sustain his habits.

In our particular drama, I thought Doug had systematically begged and borrowed from just about everyone and that I would somehow be exempt. I never expected that our characters would share dialogue on life's same page.

I was wrong.

I had lived in Los Angeles for nearly two decades and could count on one hand the number of times I had interacted with my brother since settling into my life in California. Quite honestly, I thought little about him except for the occasional mention of him from my mother on our weekly telephone calls. Those calls were always generated by me. That's why receiving a call from her on my fairly new flip phone felt strange and foreign. Her voice sounded frantic.

"Your brother is there—in Los Angeles. You have to go help him!" she pleaded.

"Where?" I questioned.

"Somewhere on Sunset Boulevard," she answered. "He called and told me he had taken a bus there. He's sleeping on the streets. Please! You've got to go help him!"

It was rare that my mother took the initiative to call and I had not heard my mom this rattled in a while. All those adolescent jealousies of how she loved Doug the most—he was the first born male child, he was the sports hero, the one she had been able to brag about to everyone—came flooding back at me.

"Mom, Sunset goes on for miles and miles. I gotta have more info than that."

She relayed some landmark that he had mentioned and at least it narrowed my field of searching to a three-block radius in the heart of Hollywood.

I got in the car and headed that way. What was I supposed to do with him once I found him? I wondered.

I was scheduled to be a keynote speaker the next evening at a conference in Austin, Texas and my plane was to leave at 6:30 in the morning. I could not miss this conference. My entire predicted monthly income was derived from this event.

My stomach churned and tightened at the thought of missing the work and at what unexpected developments awaited me at the sight of a brother I hadn't seen or talked to in years. I found the landmark my mother mentioned and drove as slowly as traffic would permit, peering down the side streets for any signs of this man that felt like a complete stranger. I circled back, parked the car, and got out. I glanced between buildings and finally, down an alleyway, I saw him. Bundled up in a coat, and sitting with his back against a brick wall, was my brother.

"Doug, it's David," I called out.

Upon seeing me, he started to stand. The once tall, larger-than-life figure seemed hunched over, his skin was leathery and burnt, his right hand clutched an over-stuffed suitcase.

He started to cry.

His voice drenched with remorse, he let go a stream of apologies that flooded from his lips.

"It's okay," I said, "We'll figure something out."

Truth be told, I hadn't a clue where to begin.

Every phone call to local substance abuse facilities turned up futile. No one had a free bed. Every recommendation from one only led to the same story from another—no room. I was resigned to the fact that I wasn't going anywhere until I found a place for him to detox.

My internal voices began. "Maybe I could just leave him at my place. Go do the conference and come right back."

"Are you nuts!? He's admitted taking combinations of 25 to 30 muscle relaxants/amphetamines a day in combination with whatever else he could get his hands on. Do you realize what he'll do to your place when he needs more?"

My anger and resentment began to rise. Here I was placed with an opportunity to practice love and compassion, towards a blood brother no less, and I resented being put in this position. I hated what he had done to himself. I hated the way he had cheated my mom out of money, hurt his children. Then, as if resurrecting some ancient, transferable, childlike fear, I wondered what he might do to me if his need for medicated relief became too strong.

Finally, a local facility recommended the Salvation Army in the skid-row section of downtown Los Angeles. The drill was to line up at 6:30 a.m. and go through an intake. If there was a bed, you were allowed to stay there for 21 days. That would buy me some time till another bed opened. I made the call and cancelled my conference appearance.

I didn't sleep a wink that night. Just knowing he was out there in the living room, on the couch, kept me on pins and needles.

The next morning, freshly showered and with enough belongings and toiletries to get him situated, we drove towards downtown. Doug stared out the passenger side window as we made our way through the neighborhoods of Los Angeles. We barely spoke to one another yet my mind chatter was racing with questions to ask him. I longed to know how it all came to this.

When and why do any of us make such decisive turns in our human dramas that we could go from experiencing the pinnacle of record-breaking success to sleeping in alleys off Sunset Boulevard? I truly wanted to know yet could not muster the courage to ask.

It was brisk that morning and my hands were shoved in my pockets for warmth. I kept telling him not to worry, that I would figure something out while he got clean. I avoided saying too much lest I spark some flammable emotional outburst or provoke him to take off and run.

Advancing to the front of the line, he was accepted and I felt a sense of relief, albeit temporary.

Within days, his remorseful demeanor soon gave way to demanding phone calls, wanting money and cigarettes. His detox experience brought out every conceivable story to try and enroll me in getting him out or providing him with a temporary loan. He told me how much physical pain he was in. He told me there were more drugs easily accessible on the inside of this place and that he would be better off staying with me.

One request he offered was actually viable. He gave me the name of a man associated with the Major League Baseball Association and demanded I tell him where he was. I questioned what good that would do since he hadn't played in years. He kept insisting.

I called and tracked down the man Doug mentioned who seemed well aware of my brother's ongoing situation. He asked that I give him 24 hours to figure out a solution. The next day he called back, relaying he had a one-way ticket waiting for my brother at the airport. They would deliver him to a state-of-the-art rehab facility in Florida. There, he could stay for up to three months, receive proper medical care and in-depth psychological treatment. He would then be given opportunities for work placement programs as well as a place to live. They would continue to offer professional counseling and strive to help him turn his life around.

"Sheesh," I thought, "he must have a monopoly on silver platters." I had this dichotomous swirl of feelings from being happy for him mixed with anger that his solutions seemed so swift and effortless. It seems once you've been a professional athlete, no matter what befalls you, the national organization will find ways to support you in getting back on your feet. My job was to simply get him on the plane.

After repacking his suitcase, I picked him up from the Salvation Army and began the drive to the Los Angeles airport. We rode in silence. He stared out the side window, nervously tapping his leg. Finally, I couldn't help but say to him, "Doug, do you realize what an amazing gift you have been given?"

He sullenly shook his head.

That was in 1999, before 9/11, and I was able to escort him to the gate and watch him as he boarded for Florida. He never turned around to wave. He simply merged with the rest of the passengers and disappeared down the Jetway. With a sigh of both relief and remorse, I headed back for my car.

"Well I guess that little drama is over with, AND I still haven't a clue what it was really about."

As I drove home, I felt this persistent voice keep questioning me.

"David, what is your greatest fear?"

"What?"

"What is your greatest fear?"

As I really pondered the question, I began to focus back on the knot in my stomach that had been overlooked by all the adrenaline of the situation—the income I was losing from the cancelled conference.

"You wanna know what the biggest, darkest fear is?" I shouted to the air. "I'll tell you. It's winding up on the streets."

There. I'd said it. All that loyalty to lack that came from a childhood filled with uncertainty. Listening to my widowed mother repeat over and over again that that's where we might wind up had settled securely in the very DNA of my bones. I had created it to be the horror of horrors, one that I would spend the rest of my life trying to avoid.

BOOM—it hit me.

"Oh, my God. Don't you get it?" the voice questioned. "That's just what happened to Doug! He showed up and played out your biggest fear. In glorious human . . . flesh . . . Technicolor . . . reality . . . he lived out your worst nightmare. And what happened? He was totally taken care of. I mean REALLY taken care of." The voice continued, "If it could happen for him (being cared for), do you have the slightest doubt that it could happen for you? And do you honestly think it will ever get that far? Why don't you just drop the fear once and for all and make room for something better?"

That awareness has empowered me for years afterwards.

Doug took his own life two days before Christmas in 2004. He had left a note for a new wife that simply said, "Check the car." In the front seat of that car, in a driveway somewhere in Tarpon Springs, Florida, he used a gun to help him make his exit. I had not seen or spoken to him since that morning drive to the airport. He had not shown up for either of my sister's funerals and we guessed that things had not improved. His drama was of a magnitude I will never comprehend and he played his part with choices vastly different than mine.

I trust his soul is at peace now.

As far as my own drama? Well, it took my brother to show me in person how to change the course of it—to play my part in life more consciously—to teach me that I actually had nothing to fear, that the now clichéd quote that we have nothing to fear but fear itself is truly a mainstay for all our lives. I would always be taken care of. My job is not lingering in the fear that it may not be so. I would have liked to thank him for this profound awareness in person but I trust now that as he waits in the wings for his next entrance, he knows.

P.S.: Condolences and e-mails continued to arrive over the years, stories from young adults who said how Doug had taken the time to autograph a shirt, a card, a glove, or bat with such grace and presence. One young girl shared how Doug had gone out of his way to buy and send her brother a glove and ball after writing him about his hardship with leukemia. Many talked of their signed baseball cards and how that opening day game for Toronto will forever live in their hearts.

Over time our perceptions shift and we become aware that just because people are unable to express love or compassion in one avenue of their lives does not mean they are totally void of those traits. Doug was fiercely loyal to many of his fans and made an indelible impression with them and in the sport of baseball.

1) The revelation my brother Doug brought to my awareness is what I term My Big Lie. My big lie was a very primal belief that I would wind up on the street. Regardless of whatever successes came my way, this primal belief was an imminent and probable outcome. Doug "lived it out" to show me its fallacy. Are you able to articulate what your big lie might be?

2) Why can you call such a limited belief a lie? What actions can you "live out" to show that this belief has no power over you other than what you give it?

3) My perception of Doug and his soul's mission has shifted over the years. Rather than seeing his life as a waste, I see it as a teacher offering me an intricate and powerful gift. It is a humbling transition in belief. Are there those in your life who have lived seemingly wasted existences and yet, in hindsight, their behaviors brought you tremendous lessons? What does that say about the value of every life?

Lather, Rinse, Repeat

> It takes courage . . . to endure the sharp pains of
> self-discovery rather than choose to take the dull
> pain of unconsciousness that would last the rest
> of our lives.

> – Marianne Williamson

"God give me strength," a woman sighed in the beginning
of class.

I gathered she still carried some belief that strength
was a quality outside of herself, something held in reserve
by a dualistic God for special times. She broke down in
frustration, her voice shaking as she spoke about her fifty-
plus-year struggle with being overweight. Her memories
of being "abnormal" started as early as the age of three.
She had calculated that throughout her years on the dieting
journey she had gained and lost nearly 1000 pounds. When
she experienced a thinner frame, better jobs had appeared
and being "loved" had surfaced, giving her a glimpse of its
possibility. When she regained the weight, the jobs would
evaporate, much like the affections of the world. The return

to her undesirable state, as she called it, had left her with an undercurrent of impenetrable futility. Yet here she was, week after week, in another spiritual class, looking at spiritual principles, even voicing spiritual affirmations.

The class was geared around the fundamentals of building a healing consciousness. Her attendance told me there was still some semblance of hope that within her existed the possibility for self-love and happiness.

She elaborated on how much of her association with getting and receiving love had been woven into the amount she weighed. Her mother had constantly berated her about her looks as a child and she felt her mother's withholding of affection as an indication that her appearance was the reason. Her solution: fix the appearance, get the love.

I pointed out her initial comment and its reference to a God outside of her. Did she really think the strength was somewhere up there? I asked her to revisit the principle of an Intelligence not separate from but within her. Could any part of her lifelong struggle be relieved in embracing the concept of non-duality?

This concept reveals that there are not "two" powers in our Universe. There is only one Universal power which is the indwelling Intelligence within all life. This "Allness" included her whether she acknowledged Its presence or not. Within her body is a heart. She does not need to ask the heart to beat. The intelligence within every bodily system knows precisely what to do and so the heart beats because we have no resistance to this intelligence. You can't see the intelligence itself but you can see its handiwork. She has the authority to disrupt this intelligence with abusive, neglectful acts, thoughts, and beliefs. Likewise, within her is an innate sense of resilience—the strength she was requesting. The strength knows exactly what to do as well as when and how to do it. All that is required of her is to let that strength rise up in her awareness and not resist it—not disown or doubt its presence. You can't see the strength itself but, again, you can see its handiwork. She has the authority to disrupt this strength by dwelling in critical, neglectful thoughts and self-abusing behavior.

If she desires strength in any given situation, she must recognize that strength is already there within her. You don't look for strength, strength just is. The same applies to love. Let us stop looking for love and open our eyes to the love all around us. The great minister and motivator Michael Beckwith often states, "You do not go out and make something happen. You go out and let something happen."

Yet so many of us continue to look for validation "out there." Life is lived in a somewhat desperate game of hopscotch, jumping from one quick fix to the next in hopes of repairing a fractured sense of self. We grow more anxious, more separate, compounding the illusion that people can diminish the quality of our lives by withdrawing their love. No one has the power to make us feel any particular way other than the way we choose to feel. If we give our power away to anyone or anything to justify our value, there will always be a price to pay in physical and emotional coin tantamount to the approval of a fickle world. Thus, to try and stay worthy of love in that manner is a journey of anxious preoccupation. Writer Anaïs Nin penned, "Anxiety is love's greatest killer. It makes others feel as you might when a drowning man holds on to you. You want to save him, but you know he will strangle you with his panic."

For the woman in class to repeatedly use language and thought in building a belief that she is weak, incapable, and powerless just keeps all her inherent power in mental storage. Instead, she could commit to rewording and reshaping her experience by affirming, "Strength is within me and it courses through my every breath, resonates in my every word, and powerfully appears in my every action, all in perfect timing and unfailing precision."

There is a remarkable difference in energy between her opening line and the affirmation suggested.

With her permission, those attending the class began to dialogue about all of her "God" qualities. Her fellow students went around and simply spoke the truth about her—her beautiful inner light, her smile, her amazing work ethic, her sense of humor, the beauty of her shimmering silvered hair.

"Enough!" she softly laughed through tears. The familiarity of her cycle of rejection was deeply embedded and this audible outpouring of love was bringing up a vulnerability she was not ready to feel. She was accustomed to walking and talking the path of the lonely misfit. We gave her space. We faithfully invited her into subsequent class discussions but she began to gradually withdraw. I believe she knew her unworthiness would not be fed in this setting and she was not ready to let it starve.

Even though she physically left the class her presence lingered. Her behavior caused a surge of discussion and conscious decision-making among the dozen who saw themselves in her fear. It was as if she had played proxy to what their lives might look like if they chronically neglected their true inner beings and continued running from one quick fix to the next.

They did not want to fight, flee, or freeze anymore. They made an intentional vow to take sincere action.

That vow resurrected an incident from my past. Years ago I happened to glance at the back of a shampoo bottle. Perhaps it was some great smell wafting from the suds that caused my curiosity to see what the actual ingredient might be. I honestly don't remember the motive but I do remember being amused at the end line of the product instruction. *Lather, Rinse, Repeat.*

I thought to myself, how many actually repeat the process? And I was at once thunderstruck at the parallel to our own personal growth process. Here was Spirituality 101 offered up on a bottle of shampoo.

Lather

In our exploration for personal meaning and our relationship with consciousness, we must return to the fundamental questions of "who am I?" and "why am I here?" To embark upon finding answers to such questions is comparable to opening the shampoo bottle and lathering up. It's an intention to seek a bigger experience than the one we are presently having. It's answering an inherent calling to cleanse ourselves of the dense human impediments we wear.

But an even greater memorable discovery on the path of lathering by my students was perhaps to first answer a more important question: Where am I?

In the beginning, we might attempt to give a geographical answer but eventually we find ourselves with this familiar response, "I am in the Universe."

But what exactly is the Universe? Is it just planets and stars, galaxies and constellations? Or, like all things, does the study of the cosmos also have more to it than just its measurables?

Ernest Holmes, one of the most influential American spiritual writers of the twentieth century, described the Universe as the Cosmic World, a perfect patterning, where One Power alone acts. The One Power, called by many names—Originating Intelligence, God, Source—is self-evident in its creation. This self-evident Power is perfect order, perfect design. If the Universe were not perfect, It could not exist for a single moment. From this premise, Holmes deduced that if the Universe is a perfect system, then everything in It must be perfect. So the answer to the question "where am I?"—from a spiritual cosmological viewpoint—would be a Perfect Universe inhabited by perfect people. The "who am I?" would be a perfect being and the "why am I here?" would be to express that perfection.

That analysis might be one of the hardest ideologies for any of us ever to accept.

Not only are most individuals unable to see or cast themselves in such a glimmering light but it is rare for most of us to sustain a belief that anyone else within our circle of influence is this embodiment of perfection as well.

What is perfection? If we caged that word into simply meaning physical flawlessness, then that kind of perfection is the elusive butterfly we keep trying to catch with a torn net. That kind of perfection is a warped human ideal that fluctuates and morphs as fast as the changing trends created within the world's advertising machines to keep us buying more of what we supposedly need. By that definition, physical perfection is impossible. Our emotional actions and reactions to the world around us are also a progressive learning process that teeter totter between success and mistake, turmoil and joy, bitterness and love, addiction and sobriety. Nothing that any of us would consider perfect.

So what is this spiritual cosmological perfection that Ernest Holmes was referring to?

The perfection of each of us has nothing to do with our physical persona or our emotional state. The perfection of each of us is our soul. It is the essence of who we are. It is our truth. These physical and emotional trappings are the instruments we get to work with in this lifetime to give more of that true essence room to breathe. "We are," as Pierre Teilhard de Chardin said, "spiritual beings having a human experience."

Consider that the examination of life is comparable to spiritual archeology. We may dig through layers of dirt to uncover our buried truth residing under layers and layers of false domestication. We may even have made the unconscious decision to stay buried to shield ourselves from illusional enemies and self-chosen fears. Yet, as Holmes described, we are perfect spiritually. The degree to which we are willing to lather and wash our earthly imperfections is the degree to which more of our inherent wholeness may finally be brought to light.

Over the years, throughout countless teaching experiences, the hang-up with the word perfection only grew in resistance. Yet to say "our true nature is wholeness" received dramatically greater welcoming than the use of the word perfection.

Students could relate to how they were mistakenly looking for others to make them whole because of the dedicated focus to their flaws. Students could relate to how easily they were swayed by the next big advertised thing to bring them happiness due to a belief that they were fractured or incomplete.

Perhaps it isn't about "perfection" vs. "wholeness," but our feeling associated with the words. All too frequently I am in conversation with those whose wounds of religiosity are continuously picked at by the use of the word God. If I refer to the "All" as Creator or Source, then their heads nod approvingly and they are receptive to the conversation.

The lesson here is that it isn't about the brand of shampoo (perfection vs. wholeness). It's about being willing to open the bottle and start the lathering process to clean away the blockages to our wholeness.

Rinse

It would be rather silly to step out of the shower with a head full of suds and proceed with our day. It feels equally as silly to establish working at dislodging our identities from the grime of our false stories, make attempts to shake up our fears of less than, or even go so far as to create intentions of returning to our wholeness only to do nothing about any of it. To have lathered all this up without taking the time to rinse away the density of those excuses is a continued waste of our time.

I have seen many others like the woman in the beginning of the story show up steadily over the years in all shapes, sizes, ages, and gender. Some of these folk talk big, earnest talk, even to the point of class conversation domination, but they have no interest in doing the internal work required to let go of one limiting belief. When called out about that, they seem to realize they've used this group up with their stories and have to move on and find another one. Others sit quietly, week after week, their nonparticipation feeling counter-intuitive to our topics of spiritual mastery and our relationship to the laws of the Universe. Some sit with arms folded in an energy of "prove it to me" and with all of them I simply inquire, "Why are you here?"

The answers tend to be similar. "I like the information. This stuff intrigues me."

Yet intrigue needs a little cooperation. One must rinse all that lathering away.

Rinsing is letting go. Not so much letting go of the story but letting go of the identification you have created about yourself regarding the story—like the classic, "who would I be without my pain?"

Who would I be without my label of abandoned housewife or unemployable alcoholic or fibromyalgia diagnosis or irritable bowel disease or failed business owner or cancer or . . .

Michael Singer, in his book *The Untethered Soul*, writes, "Billions of things could happen that you haven't even thought of yet. The question is not whether they will happen. Things are going to happen. The real question is whether you want to be happy regardless of what happens."

To rinse is to say "no matter what, I choose to release any and all dualistic held beliefs that label me separate, unworthy, or damaged." Rinsing allows us the space to experience the fundamental principle of happiness regardless of any past, present, or future circumstance that may appear to the contrary. Letting go gives birth to genuine joy because we finally realize that joy, happiness, and contentment are never dependent upon circumstance. I can be happy regardless of whatever earthly malady has come my way. Happiness is simply a choice.

Repeat

The quality of our lives is a reflection of the quality of our thoughts. Measure for measure, they echo back exactly what we negatively or joyously shout out into a subjective canyon of impartial receptivity.

How uncomfortable or unhappy do we have to be before we reach an irrepressible desire to faithfully "shout" ourselves out of the beliefs of separation and see that the answers already exist within us, where we continually affirm and see our alignment with "I *am* strength" rather than "God give me strength"?

When the desire for change becomes strong enough, then it is simply a matter of training—even more accurately, re-training our minds to re-welcome what it is that our divine soul already knows is true. This re-training does not have to be held in the light of difficulty. We have trained all our lives. We trained to walk, talk, steady a spoon from bowl to mouth, tie our shoes, tell time . . .

When we look back on these accomplishments do we declare, "Oh, that was so traumatic, so difficult!" No, we learned these things because they brought us freedom to progress in our world. It was important enough for us to learn and master them. The training for their mastery seems absolutely logical. Does our spiritual freedom not carry the same importance and logic?

I remember motivational author Marianne Williamson saying, "There is no difference in difficulty between healing a paper cut and healing cancer. It's just that we believe there is."

There is no higher degree of difficulty in learning how to tie a shoe than there is in removing the pattern of negative thinking. How do we stop talking about changing and actually do something about it?

We have to want to.

We unconsciously mimic others who expend tremendous energy in trying to control this self-imposed separate force. Whether by fighting, fleeing, or freezing up, we obey the fear of being left without. And by obeying this thought patterning we are served a life experience of emotional and physical segregation—like a solitary island, even though John Dunne and his poem encouraged otherwise.

We have to feel we deserve the freedom that comes with the change. We have to know that we can handle our greatness.

We wouldn't be here—on this planet, in this body, at this time—if we couldn't handle the greatness of our divine destinies. Otherwise, why would we have chosen to come and have this earthly experience?

We *lather*—we show up with good intentions of wanting to get rid of the heaviness and grime that weigh us down. We take classes, go on retreats, sit on the therapist's chair, but how many take it to the next levels of rinsing away all that doesn't serve and then repeating the practice as often and as long as necessary to gain a new level of self-awareness?

Many years later as I write about this particular class and this particular woman, I am entertained with the idea of how wonderfully synchronistic everything turned out to be. It was in that group that many of the pieces of the grand cosmic puzzle were revealed, discussed, and implemented equally among all with a clarity and conviction I had never witnessed. They each were ready to show up (lather) and make an earnest vow to stay faithful to the process. They each were ready to let go of (rinse) the false and petty ideas that had caused them so much restriction, and they were willing to engage in spiritual practice (repeat) as long as necessary to begin to align with their greater purpose. Those remaining students were a priceless combination of equally intentioned souls who were only made aware of just how united they were in their hunger through this woman's sharing and resistant behavior. I like to believe her presence was not random but that the soul of her showed up and played out her part in a long-held agreement with the rest of them.

Spiritual mastery simply takes repetitive training—immersion into a new state of awareness by course correcting our habitual negatives into habitual positives.

We train our minds to absorb language, mobility, skills, parenting, talents—the same applies for our thoughts—and we train ourselves to drop those that tell a different story than the one our souls know as true. Soon, the training becomes instinctual just as dropping a hot potato becomes instinctual.

One powerful practice I call The Drop and Give Me Twenty exercise is what I give students who say they're serious about repeating their practice. It goes like this: When you think a limited, self-loathing, or worry-filled thought about yourself, drop it immediately—just like a hot potato—and give voice to twenty things about you that are great, unique, and special.

1. I am wonderfully detailed in my work and do an excellent job with my assignments.

2. I am an excellent cook and make wonderful dishes that bring "oohs" and "ahs" to everyone who partakes of them.

3. I have a wonderful artistic eye for decorating and can create beautiful environments.

4. I am a wonderful listener and people feel seen and heard in my presence.

5. I have beautiful eyes.

6. I have a sharp mind that loves to problem solve.

7. I am a responsible driver.

8. I have a beautiful singing voice.

9. I know how to make a great cup of coffee.

10. I appreciate waiters and waitresses and tip generously.

11. I am blessed with a great head of hair.

12. I would make an excellent film critic because many people like my cinematic opinions.

13. I can powerfully express my feelings through poetry and songwriting.

14. I love my sense of adventure and willingness to try new things.

15. I am articulate and well-read.

16. There are a lot of great milestones that I have completed in my life and I give myself credit for completing them.

17. I am kind to my animals.

18. I am willing to be equally kind to the members of my family whether they offer that back or not.

19. Just the fact that I am doing this exercise means that I must care enough about myself to let my true greatness break through.

20. I am enough.

. . . and on and on and on.

People will often complain about this exercise. "Twenty is too much! Why can't it just be one?"

By having to name so many positive things about yourself in each momentary conscious engagement, you spend more time exploring and immersing your mind in a different pattern of energy. You begin demanding an entirely different set of living standards by immediately choosing to move into the realm of conscious affirmation. You don't just sit in the self-deprecating idea and allow it to linger within you. You take dominion over your thoughts. This repetitive spiritual practice makes us aware that every minute of every day can be an ongoing focus on our good qualities. And, with each day, the training ushers in its reciprocal reward through our outer world conditions. The more you focus on your true essential qualities of unique greatness, the more the world matches you in that recognition. The training brings on an exhilaration, much like a musician feels after continued practice on a composition. The details of our lives take on an ease—our abundance seems effortless, our physical stability and energy improves. Our relationships improve as well and the palpable quality of this earthly experience is a joyous one.

I remember reading in Ernest Holmes' earlier works where he mentioned that if we did this kind of dedicated, conscious thought work regarding ourselves every day without fail for one year, at the end of that year we would not recognize ourselves.

And so we return to lathering some more, rinsing some more, and repeating always.

That formula for a better life that everyone is wanting? There it is.

1) What do you believe to be the ultimate freedom in the concept of non-duality?

2) The Ernest Holmes' reference depicting how "the Universe is perfect, therefore everything in it must be perfect" indicates that you are perfect. Can you describe any resistance you feel around such a statement? What basic personal beliefs would you need to drop in order to make that statement a reality? Do you want to? If not, why?

3) The Lather, Rinse, Repeat process can be summarized as recognizing and loosening our grip on limiting ideas, cleansing those ideas from our identities, and continuously repeating the process for as long as we are alive. How have you successfully used such a practice in transcending negative patterning? What major areas can you apply this spiritual practice to in your current circumstances?

Kilimanjaro

> With a hint of good judgment, to fear nothing, not
> failure or suffering or even death, indicates that you
> value life the most. You live to the extreme; you
> push limits; you spend your time building legacies.
> Those do not die.
>
> — Criss Jami

"Ah, American. Chuck Norris!" exclaims the young
Tanzanian man behind the plexiglass registration booth.
"Jambo! Jambo!"

It is the second time after seeing my American passport
and my freshly grown beard that locals tell me I look like the
movie/television star and it will not be the last. Perhaps it
is the low hanging bags under my eyes that accompany the
beard that moved me from what used to be a sort of Vic
Damone, George Clooney kind of doppleganger to, umm,
well, Chuck.

It takes us an hour and a half to drive from the city
of Arusha to the entrance of the Machame route, one of
seven trails that await the adventuring climber to make an

attempt to reach the summit of Mt. Kilimanjaro. Although one of the most scenic and best trails to help the climber acclimatize due to its zigzag patterning, it also holds some of the greatest challenges in ascending the world's tallest freestanding mountain—a much publicized title offering boasting rights to the country and the climber based on the geological distinction that the entire base is separate from any other mountain range.

The early August air is cool and moist, a slight temperature drop from what greeted us earlier as we exited the hotel. A persistent drizzle makes the pen used to sign our names slippery in my fingers and causes the pages in the registration ledger to warp like a thick stack of lasagna noodles.

Mark, a longtime friend whose adventurous spirit matches my own, agreed to attempt the climb with me. And now that our initial journeying across the globe brings us to this starting point, we are introduced to the rest of our climbing companions, Jon (pronounced *Yahn*), a 59-year-old retired South African lawyer from Johannesburg and Gideon, a 39-year-old marketing consultant, also South African but currently working in Dubai.

We are instructed to carry our day packs with only the essentials, mostly water, rain gear, and walking poles, and the rest of our gear and supplies are taken and squeezed into large canvas duffle bags that porters stand ready to transport.

The moment is finally here. We are greeted by our guide, Harold—youthful, short in stature, and remarkably poised. He began doing this kind of work ten years prior, first as a porter, then working his way up to chief guide, and now at 35 he has traversed every trail and memorized every step after having "summited" close to two hundred times.

We simply start to walk, following Harold. Within minutes we enter a landscape of low-hanging fog. It is a rainforest with lush ferns that at times create a towering canopy over the trail. Indigenous trees covered with lichen and varieties of low-hanging moss hit us in the face as we start to ascend the slippery steps of rock, wood, and gravel.

Porters carrying everything from overflowing baskets to duffels filled with gear to jugs of water and food supplies balanced atop their heads begin passing us swiftly, and I mean swiftly.

"How in the world can they do that?" I question, all moving with speed and agility but also feeling every ounce of their cargo by the strained look on their faces.

I begin noticing that I am feeling somewhat guilty. I have a simple daypack, perhaps all of 15 pounds. Each porter's load is significantly heavier, perhaps five times as much with everything from tents and poles to water jugs and food supplies.

It is a feeling I am to wrestle with every day.

It is necessary to watch every step for there is no part of the path that isn't covered with every size rock imaginable. The zigzag patterning begins and we move from left to right then back again like obedient ants traveling upwards into the dense fog.

Curious, I want to pick my head up more and take in the view. After all, I am in an African rainforest. But it is a luxury I have to avoid since every step has to be deliberate.

I feel good. Even with ascending consistently, my breathing stays normal, the damp air seems to keep everyone cool, and I am thinking, "You got this, David. You got this."

Several hours later, our beginning rhythm leads to our first meal on the trail. Rounding a curve there is a folding table with four chairs. We are served unidentifiable sandwiches cut in half, orange slices, mango, and pineapple juice. The four of us chat. Jon is climbing to celebrate his 60th birthday that very week. He is also letting his law practice go and trying his hand at growing pomegranates. Gideon fancies himself a jock and also plans to propose to his girlfriend at the very top by writing "Will you marry me?" on a small whiteboard he has brought along for the big photo opportunity on Uhuru Peak. Mark and I? Well, after 30-plus years of friendship, we discovered we shared the same adventuresome spirit mixed with a side of crazy, an ever-increasing desire to challenge ourselves, and a hunger to see the world. After walking the Camino de Santiago four years ago, Kilimanjaro was one of the next things on our collective bucket list.

Harold beckons us to finish so we can continue on. We have at least another four hours before reaching our first camp.

Still climbing, still climbing, our pace becomes slower.

Somewhere in the next couple of hours, my upper thighs start to twinge. The consistency of motion is causing them to cramp. Gideon begins feeling nauseated and Mark is not feeling all that great either. Around 7,000 feet, the first adjustment in altitude starts kicking in. Jon, the oldest, looking at all of us with a curmudgeonly sense of disbelief, has barely broken a sweat.

Stopped, Harold reaches in his gear bag and pulls out some BenGay type ointment for me to rub on my thighs. He urges the other guys to drink water.

The temperature is starting to drop but we are all too soaked with sweat to notice.

Another two hours and my thighs quiet down. Gideon gets worse. "I can't believe it!" he bellows. "The first day and this is happening."

He starts to blame Dubai and its high heat and lack of mountains for the reason why he is suffering. His head is pounding and he can barely contain his tears.

Harold motions for his second-in-command, a tall, quiet African man named John (pronounced the English way), to continue with the three of us and we leave Harold with Gideon.

Coming out of the rainforest into more rugged terrain, we finally reach our first night's camp named the same as the trail, Machame. The porters have long set up everything including a tent for dining. Standing at the level of the clouds, a jutting cliff provides the base for the camp and makes quite a stunning landscape and the late sun seems to paint everything with a Maxfield Parrish hue. Second-in-command John shows us to our sleeping tents which will become our collapsing space each night. Mark and I share a tent that feels the size of two coffins pushed together with the lids open. It is tight, especially with our porter-carried gear inside with us as well.

There must be about 70 tents in all, scattered around this first night's camp at 9,400 feet above sea level.

Gideon and Harold show up almost an hour later. Harold has talked him off the emotional ledge and coaxed him to reach camp.

We are given plastic wash bins of hot water to clean our hands and then as the sun is setting we gather for dinner.

Both Gideon and Mark are feeling nauseated. The evening meal of a porridge type soup, bread, and some pieces of fried fish goes mostly uneaten.

By 8:30 it is dark and the sound of multi-language conversation can be heard throughout the sea of tents. It is our first true taste of cold and both Mark and I have already adjusted and readjusted the contents of the tent in order to get our sleeping bags to lie completely flat. A padded floor mat for cushioning helps but you know you are just beginning to introduce your back to the indignities of nature's unrelenting mattress.

Mark and I talk of the day, mostly whispering, since the mountain air seems to amplify one's voice. We can hear Gideon say, "I feel better! I feel better!" apparently receiving some relief from medication from the crew for his early onset altitude sickness.

"I wish I could say the same," whispers Mark.

"You will," I answer. "Maybe during the night your body will acclimate and the nausea will disappear by morning."

Within minutes, he sits straight up and reaches for the zipper of the tent door. Barely getting it open, he begins to heave his guts out onto the dirt in front of the tent.

"Someone's sick, someone's sick!" chant those inside the tents around us.

Harold comes over and respectfully takes a stick and begins sweeping the pool of vomit away from the tent door as the dirt absorbs it.

Pale and shaken, Mark feels the relief he's longed for all afternoon.

Sipping water, he looks over at me, a bit surprised by the suddenness of what just happened.

"You all right?" I ask.

"I think so," he replies between sips.

"Dinner and drinks," he follows.

"What?"

"Dinner and drinks," he repeats. "The next time you call me to talk me into something, it better be for dinner and drinks."

Laughing, our breath visible in the cold, we welcome some much needed sleep on this first night on the mountain.

~~~~~~~~

It is the best cup of tea I've ever had. The blue plastic mug filled with a highly potent brew of ginger burns the back of my throat as I drink but I don't really mind.

"Asante sana," I say to the porter who walks to each tent offering the morning brew.

81

The thick tea is hot, perfect for the bone cold chill running through my body now exposed to its first morning in the elements following a long sleepless night.

Just before retiring the night before, Jon (Yahn) noticed a brazen rat running around our tent entrance. I had an open ziplock bag with protein bars sitting on top of my day pack and the rat was standing on its hind legs, whiskers shaking, calculating how to climb up and investigate the smell. I shooed him away.

All night I heard, felt (maybe imagined) a persistent scurrying around my head on the other side of the tent material. My thoughts went immediately to the rat and I imagined he was circling the tent, perhaps calling friends, and plotting how best to overtake us and gain access to those luxury bars that had traveled halfway around the world. I decided to sleep with a hat on.

All that imagining kept me up, tossing, rolling, adjusting in the confines of the sleeping bag in hopes of discovering the perfect position. One helpful thought was that if they were rats—a thriving community of them, let's say—then there couldn't be anything *larger* out there lurking in the darkness unless that larger something was taking a vow of abstinence from predation.

Before breakfast, you must repack your gear, refill your water containers and purify the contents, and then with fingers crossed, have a diplomatic conversation with your bowels about how much you would appreciate cooperation from them while here at the camp. Granted, the bathroom situation was still primitive—a choice between the "how low can you go" squatting hole or the elevated bowl which you still cannot sit on because the rim is molded out of jagged concrete. For added athleticism, there is the fact that you are wearing multiple layers of clothing which must be mathematically maneuvered for effective results.

My windbreaker is covered in frost as well as the rag provided for me to wash my hands every morning and evening at camp. I learn quickly that you can't leave "laundry" hanging on the tent lines overnight.

After a breakfast of porridge, toast, and orange slices, we are suited up and ready to begin the day's ascent.

This second day continues through increasingly sparse trees and bushes into what is known as the moorlands. Remnants of permafrozen tundra mixed with patches of thawed scree are the most common terrain. I remember overhearing that the Machame route was definitely the most scenic but you would not have gathered that from today's view. Still walking through low-lying mist, the lack of sleep from the night before seems to make today's trek feel far more arduous than day one.

For more than seven hours we climb, stopping only for water, a brief lunch, and some more psychological coaching from Harold. It is a tough, monotonous day that delivers us to Shira Camp and more majestic views above the clouds. We are now at approximately 12,500 feet above sea level. Even though none of us feel like it, we are encouraged to drop our gear inside our already arrived tents and walk another 30 minutes up to the Shira Caves. The last thing you want to do is climb more after arriving at camp, but this little mini hike ritual is designed to help climbers internally acclimatize even more, having you go up and then come down before sleeping.

From Shira Camp we have a direct view of Mount Meru, the topographic centerpiece of Arusha National Park. For a brief time before sunset, the view is clear and the evening colors once again seem like an impressionistic painting. My gaze is broken by the arrival of my basin of hot water. Face and hands are washed, dinner of stew meat and boiled pasta is served, and the four of us eat in quiet.

We all look at each other, silently questioning our sanity. "The pride lasts long after the pain ends," I remember Jon saying earlier when describing his experiences as a long-distance runner.

Still trusting I will find my rhythm in the hiking, the yawning starts, both from altitude and fatigue. I remove my mud- and dust-covered boots, crawl into the tent, and collapse onto the sleeping bag.

And the prospect of rats—I am thankfully too tired to care.

~~~~~~~~

The urge to go to the bathroom presents itself before dawn—forcefully.

I lie there pondering my options. Can I hold it till the sun comes out? If not, there is quite a bit of maneuvering and preparing before exiting the tent. The answer is no.

Must. Go. Now.

Find the headlamp to be able to see, crawl out of the sleeping bag while remaining within the same boundary lines of the width of the bag. Feel for my top layer pants. Put them on much like how my mother used to put a girdle on back in the 60's—on her back, lying on the bed, and defying gravity with every pull and stretch upwards. Next, harness the down coat which is damp from the moist air. Go from sitting up to being on all fours. Then find the inner layer zipper of the tent, tug and struggle a bit with it because the fabric is stretched so tightly, then resume sitting position, put my double layered stocking feet out the opening and navigate boots and laces.

Then . . .

After the long-awaited bathroom journey is complete, I look up and realize that the tent gymnastics are all worth it.

There in the untainted night sky is the most majestic pattern of stars I've ever been privileged to see. I cannot recall ever witnessing the constellations without some land light interference. This is beyond bright, the edges of each star clear and defined and every pattern and trail seemingly within arm's length—the Pleiades, Milky Way, Orion's Belt, all positioned in the brilliance of the southern hemisphere.

I turn off my forehead lamp, sit on a piece of lava rock, and let the heavens entertain me.

It is only a half hour before sunrise. Rather than go through the extensive undressing and redressing, I wait for morning light, smiling at the social media post I'd remember seeing on occasion that read, "I found a really old picture of you," with an illustration of an illuminating star in a vast night sky. Writer Paulo Coelho, a favorite of mine, reminds us, "We are travelers on a cosmic journey, stardust, swirling and dancing in the eddies and whirlpools of infinity. Life is eternal. We have stopped for a moment to encounter each other, to meet, to love, to share. This is a precious moment. It is a little parenthesis in eternity."

Soon with morning light, a fresh cup of ginger tea along with a breakfast of spongy pancakes, boiled eggs, and bananas, we each prepare for our third day of climbing.

Today's destination to Barranco camp follows the acclimatization principle of "climb high, sleep low," and we will aim to go above the 14,500 feet point and retreat down to around 13,066 to rest at Barranco. The trek, above the clouds, reveals the beginnings of scenic vistas and indigenous vegetation. Lava rock is everywhere and you realize that at one time, thousands of years ago, this was an active volcano.

I am captivated by a treelike plant called Senecio. From a distance it looks like a cross between a palm tree and an aloe plant. They populate the crevices throughout this region and Harold says it is one of the national symbols of Kilimanjaro and resilient in withstanding frozen temperatures with leaves that remain green all year round.

I feel rather good today. Perhaps I was given an infusion from stargazing. I am walking in front with second-in-command John. My eyes fixate on his boots, his stride, and I do my best to mimic each step. We stop frequently as the air becomes thinner and we are instructed to keep hydrating. I was gifted with a camelback water container before the trip and I love the convenience of drinking through the hose that rests along my side.

Since mid-morning, Jon is increasingly ill—dizzy, headaches, and his steps are precarious, wobbling back and forth. Jon refused to take Diamox, the highly recommended medication that helps with advanced altitude adjustments. With only eight of the normally 14.7 pounds per square inch of pressure from the surrounding air, our bodies are doing everything they can to adjust. In extreme cases, altitude sickness can have water build up in the brain and lungs, a life-threatening situation.

From the morning's beginnings until reaching Lava Tower, a massive formation created from a long ago frozen lava flow, we have eaten little, save the snacks and bars we were encouraged to carry. Lunch is awaiting us here, behind the Tower, in a tent the porters have erected. Boulders are used to hold the four corners down as the wind is quite strong. The four of us stumble inside, sitting at the makeshift table.

There is some relief knowing our remaining hours will be traveling downward towards camp and sleep.

Jon continues struggling. The sight of food nauseates him and he excuses himself.

We are hurried to finish. I realize later just how mathematical it all is. Reach a certain elevation, stay for a calculated time, then descend to maximize the body's ability to adjust.

Several hours more and we arrive at Barranco camp. The same routine of settling in begins. In the distance is a massive wall of rock. The Barranco Wall, I guess, the arduous part of the trail where balance and precision are key. I am fairly sure it is the first thing we will attempt tomorrow, thus the nickname—the Breakfast Wall. It is the portion of the climb that Mark has dreaded the most because of his fear of heights.

I decide not to ask Harold or John for clarification.

Dinner is served before twilight—some kind of stew, plus bread and mango slices. None of us are particularly hungry but they keep saying "eat, eat."

Each night upon arrival at the camps, every climber must check in at a registration booth and sign his name, statistics, guide's name, etc. in a large ledger in order to help all park personnel keep track of who makes it to where within the massive confines of Kilimanjaro National Park's 652-square-mile circumference.

This night's camp booth has electrical outlets inside. Mark has his iPhone cord and I have a dead iPhone. Perfect ingredients for cellular resurrection. We are told there are slight chances of reception, a lucky moment to text a loved one and let them know you are among the living. No one else has succeeded so far in getting through.

Our guide, Harold, does the negotiating for me with the workers in the booth and manages to get a 10 US dollar quote for a full charge. Had I requested it on my own, it would have been double that due to the "skin tax"—a term I'd never heard before. Fair skin translates to higher price quotes.

Right before retiring, I hike back to the booth and retrieve my phone. Inside are upwards of 40 phones spread out over a cot with electrical cords running every which way. What a business! If this night is any indication of how every base camp population's electronic needs might be, then these guys are highly successful at generating multiple streams of income.

~~~~~~~~

My phone reads 3:13 a.m. I fell asleep somewhere around 10 p.m. A little more than five hours—five hours of beautiful, uninterrupted sleep. It was the longest consecutive slumber I'd had since arriving in Africa. I was able to check the time from my freshly charged iPhone.

For the next three hours, I toss, turn, and ponder our upcoming morning's adventure—climbing that wall, navigating narrow ledges, ascending higher and higher.

Someone once joked, "There are old climbers, there are bold climbers, but there are no old bold climbers!" Oh, the things I sign up for.

Hours pass, morning routine completed, and we are headed toward the towering cliff.

It is straight up the wall. Hiking poles are abandoned so that hands are free to grab onto any jagged rock for leverage, balance, and hoisting. Porters miraculously ease past us with massive loads upon their heads and I can only wonder how and why. I am humbled yet again in realizing that I cannot be doing this—experiencing this climb at the basic level of comfort which I was offered—without their help. Someone is carrying my tent, someone is carrying my duffel of supplies, someone is carrying our food source . . . I have my backpack of minimal essentials.

I have no problem with the height. In fact, I love the rests that allow me to turn around and see a far-reaching vista on this clear, cold morning.

The ascent continues and I am able to manage without too much difficulty. Even the point known as "kissing rock," where you must press your body completely against the ledge to maneuver higher, doesn't feel paralyzing in the challenge. What is taxing is the endurance part of the scramble. We are climbing, and climbing, and climbing up the "wall" for several hours.

About halfway, second-in-command John notices a leak in my daypack. Sure enough, the bottom is wet and water is seeping down my backside. The camelback pouch had somehow "manifested" a strategically placed hole in the bottom center. An unknown object pierced through the outer canvas casing and into the inner water pouch. My daily ration of water now trails behind me.

"How on earth did that happen?" I ponder. Was it from leaning my back against a too-sharp rock? No, the culprit, of all things, was a pencil point. Somehow the sharpened pencil in my bag had shifted in such a way that it created the perfect pressure towards the center bottom of the pouch. There is no way to patch the leak now or to keep it from continuing to flow out all over me. I drink what is left and depend upon the others to share.

Every now and then I can hear shouting as climbers finally make it to the crest at the top of the wall.

"Great!" I think with relief, believing if I can hear them then it must be close. But in the vast mountain air, sound travels quite far. On and on we ascend, my wet tush muddier with every rest break.

By late morning, Barranco Wall is history and we enter into terrain similar to the days before.

I am starting to feel remarkably weary. Maybe it is from the tense anticipation and the enduring hours on the wall. Maybe it is the ever-increasing altitude. But I am "spent" and realize we still have to pass the Karanga River and campsite and then continue even further to Barafu to be on schedule. The doubt regarding my capabilities starts trickling in and my faith in myself slowly begins to wane.

Not having water makes me *think* of water and the *not having of it.* Funny how our minds do that. I humbly ask for sips from Mark and Harold. Upon arrival at Karanga, I am given an empty plastic bottle to use. Water purification tablets are dropped in and we fill our containers from the river. We are told it is the last source of water until after the following day's summit. Even the porters now have to carry a day and a half's supply.

An extremely rocky zone lies before us. Very little vegetation is found as the terrain becomes more inhospitable. Boulders of every size imaginable litter the fields around us. The wind is picking up and my lined fake-fur cap, purchased on sale back in the States, becomes my prized possession and is permanently pulled over my head and ears.

We arrive at Barafu. The skies are blanketed in thick fog and mists and the wind has a high-pitched howl. It is more crowded at this stop than at any place along the journey. It seems multiple trails intersect here in preparation for summit day. Tent lines crisscross one another and I have to

91

raise my legs over the stretched cords to get to Mark's and my entry way. You can hear multi-language conversations battering against one another in sound waves of excitement and anxiety. Tomorrow is the day.

We have a briefing in our dinner tent. Harold explains about the custom to leave at midnight in order to hopefully make it to the summit by sunrise.

We are full of questions.

Do we have to stick to custom? Are all of these people leaving at midnight? Can you even see the sun at the summit? Does fog preclude the view? What are our options? And on and on.

We all agree that we do not need to summit with the sunrise. If we break custom, some ancient curse will not befall us. If we leave, say at 3 a.m., the majority of the other climbers from camp will long be ahead of us and it will mean less time climbing in the dark with only headlamps for illumination.

Lastly we get our oxygen saturation levels and pulse rate checked with a contraption called a pulse ox meter. We are told if our oxygen saturation is less than 60%, we will not be able to attempt the summit. Anything less than 90% is considered low and will require supplemental oxygen. We all pass the test, with my oxygen rate scoring the highest at 94%.

I am not hungry nor can I sleep. It is barely 9 p.m. and the cacophony of voices circle this portion of the mountain with a swirling typhoon of conversation. Mark and I just look at each other and laugh. We smell. With so many layers of clothes, down jackets and such, we are a cross between the Pillsbury Dough Boy and the Michelin Tire Man.

We reminisce about walking the Camino de Santiago four years earlier, our thirty-year friendship—anything to take our minds off what is next. And slowly, camp talk settles, albeit for a brief time.

~~~~~~~~

There are days filled with unprecedented occurrences—days aligning themselves with one revelatory moment linked to another—the birth of our child, our marriage, the passing of a dear loved one, moving day, the official good-bye. We shroud these days with deep significance for they are the days when our paths become altered and everything seemingly changes.

Today is such a day.

Tea and biscuits are brought to our tent around 2:45 a.m. I hear the word biscuit and my American mind cannot help but register a visual of flour dough balls baked in the oven. These "biscuits" are packaged cookies offered with the now familiar ginger brew.

Not much fuel, it seems, for summit day but at this hour I am not complaining. The few bites and sips feel laden with effort.

We have all attempted to sleep fully dressed sans the outer down jacket. A few forced final gulps of tea and we are called to begin. Headlamps are in place. I look up and see a faint trace of bobbing lights high above. From where

I stand, the illuminated heads of earlier departers look like glow worms floating in the sky.

"How far up are they?" I question, and a wave of nausea and dread swirl in my gut.

Mark gives me a packet of disposable hand warmers, the kind that look like large tea bags. Once crunched and gripped in your hand, the inner gel inside the packets activates heat for hours. I place one within each palm inside my gloves.

We begin. Summit day has arrived.

The night before, Harold and John both came to our dinner tent to go over the specifics of our final hours of climbing. Terrain, delirium, fatigue were all topics of discussion and Harold always brought the subject back to his 100% success rate on the Machame. Other trails, he said, had been hit or miss because of a too swift rise in altitude but the Machame is methodically laid out to help the climber succeed. Then he looked at each of us with this stoic, solemn stare as if to say, "You have no choice but to make it."

A half hour in and it already feels like trouble. Scaling rock in the dark, my heart begins to pound, my body revolts, and I begin breathing with large, audible, breath-deprived gasps that echo throughout the seeming inaccessible darkness.

"You are breathing wrong!" chides Harold, as he tries to emphasize a through-the-nose-out-the-mouth technique to calm me down. It is too difficult. My body craves more oxygen than my nostrils can deliver. I try to regulate per instruction but every ascended step feels like a punch to the gut.

I reason with myself. "The first hour of every morning is always the hardest. You'll settle in. You'll settle in."

"Breathe. I am settling in. I am settling in. Breathe."

"Am. Settling. In."

The self-talk helps and even though it all feels momentarily daunting I manage to keep moving carefully up the rocky path. Several more hours up and I imagine we have now become the glow worms for those left at the camp far below.

We stop frequently. Since I am trailing behind by about five minutes, the duration of my rests are shortened. Harold and second-in-command John play switchback with the four of us, leading then trailing the rear in order to keep a close watch on each of us.

I can't feel some of the fingers on my left hand and I squeeze and bend them vigorously to prompt any circulation.

By the first glimpse of dawn, I have gone from trailing the others by five minutes to being unable to see them at all on the slopes ahead. John has taken charge of the others and Harold hangs by me, weaving from my right to my left. My lungs are burning and air bubbles from sipping water through an insulated straw make my stomach swell and ache in the thin morning air.

I stop and stare at the ground.

"You are not walking!" Harold states. "You must keep walking."

Another hour passes. I am able to comprehend that I am audibly mumbling—not formulating words, but mumbling sounds, syllables that seem to mysteriously help my process.

Another hour passes. I stop, perhaps twice, collapsing on a rock for stability and a desperate rest. My thoughts feel jumbled and all I long to do is close my eyes and lie down on the mountain. I give in and begin shutting down, eyes closed, body slumping and I instantly feel the sting of Harold's hand across my face. He slaps me. Grabbing my shoulders he speaks firmly with determined eye contact, "You cannot close your eyes! You must keep them open! You must stay awake!"

He is right. My internal mechanisms want to give up. The lack of oxygen is making me weak and drowsy. To give in will be fatal.

I stand to begin again when Harold starts yelling at me in Swahili.

"What? I'm standing!" I think or did I respond aloud? As I turn towards him, he is pointing and yelling at the sky ahead.

In less than one second, I look up to where he is pointing to see a four-ton sized boulder flying directly at us.

It resembles something straight out of a Wile E. Coyote and the Roadrunner cartoon.

They say time stands still. How accurate a description, for within what can only be a matter of two seconds, there is assessment followed by decision making, all taking place within my brain. I see the airborne boulder. To my right is a boulder of equal size along the side of the path. I fall behind it. Harold dives left.

The boulder flies directly over our heads.

There is no adrenaline rush. Thinking back, I ask myself, "How can that be?" I can only rationalize that my delirious and exhaustive state must have led my neurotransmitters to take a holiday.

Crawling back up, using my walking poles to stand erect, the only commentary I am able to muster is a flat, barely audible monotone, "Wow, avalanche."

"Not good," replies Harold, as we turn to see where it may have made a new resting place. It was divine providence that sunlight was reigning rather than low-hanging fog, otherwise we might have never seen it coming.

I later learn that once every other year or so, an avalanche occurs from the eroding, shifting soil, often resulting in fatalities.

"Keep moving," Harold says, these short, cryptic sentences becoming his current style of communicating.

We soon enter a terrain of scree—loose, sandy gravel that offers the simulation of walking up a mountain of sand. With every three steps, I slide back one, making our headway up to the summit feel completely in vain.

This is my breaking point. I practice an internal apology—offering it to all those back home who are looking to me to prove that anything is possible.

"I can't do it," I feebly whisper to Harold. I feel awash with shame.

"Yes, you can," he replies, taking my pack and beginning to push me in the small of my back towards the crest of the scree. It is a remarkably supportive gesture but it proves too awkward for both of us in navigating the quicksand-like terrain. Harold gives up, moves to the front, and grabs my gloved hand.

His hand is bare and he intertwines his fingers with mine. He starts pulling me up.

"We just need to make it to Stella Point at the top of this crest. It's the next to the last summit point. You will at least get a certificate. There you can rest."

Astonishingly, the little boy within me perks up over the fact that I may still earn something, anything after all of this.

I stare at his hand grabbing mine and I am beyond humbled as he pulls me relentlessly up.

I completely surrender.

Suddenly, his hand represents the hand of every person, spirit, energy that has ever existed—the ceaseless, supportive lifeline that was and is always there whenever any experience prompts feelings of helplessness or giving up. It is the hand of the Universe, a direct lifeline dragging, pulling, lifting me to a greater degree of sufficiency. It is, in truth, the hand of God.

I stare back at our grip and, for a brief time, forget the physical struggle.

Perhaps it is a half hour, I can't accurately assess, but Harold continues pulling, then pulling more, bringing me up the merciless terrain.

We both stumble up those final steps where we are met by blasts of harsh, frigid winds.

There is a marker indicating Stella Point. To the side is a cavelike overhang where I make my way and collapse, taking shelter from the wind.

I have resigned within me that this is good enough. It isn't Uhuru Peak, the very top summit point, but it is close.

"Get up. We must continue."

"But you said I could . . ."

"You can't stop here. You must finish."

"Harold, I can't."

"Yes, you can. You are almost there. The hardest part is over. Less than an hour. Come."

And he stretches out his hand again, lifting me up.

I realize that even though he is most likely lying about the ease, the end has to be near. Reserves I think are long used up leak out into my bloodstream with inexplicable renewal. Gleaming glacier walls line the horizon and raw, rising emotion makes its way out of me. This is the final pathway to Uhuru Peak.

Others are making their way down, passing me and offering encouragement.

"You're almost there. Congratulations."

And not long after, off in the distance, I can see the well-worn monument sign.

The other three in my group are there, finishing their photo ops with the allotted maximum of twenty minutes allowed at that elevation without supplemental oxygen.

They have only been about twenty minutes ahead all along. They, too, have each struggled significantly.

We wearily hug and high-five as they make their way back to Stella then further down to camp.

I look over at Harold. It is just us, as it is perfectly designed to be, standing at the highest point on the continent of Africa, standing on top of the world's highest freestanding mountain. Not as tall as Everest, but pretty damn tall.

I feel an overwhelming sense of pride—a strange sort of reverence and self-respect that I've never fully allowed myself to experience before. I had become determined to accomplish something that many would have felt impossible and I had not quit. There was something in that moment that assured me that any future self-doubt would be overridden with the thought, "Remember, you climbed Kilimanjaro, David. Why do you doubt your capabilities?"

"I could not have done this without you," I say to Harold as he smiles broadly.

"It's my job."

"I know, but you don't understand. I would have never made it here had it not been for you."

"It's my job," he says again.

"Yes, indeed, it is your job," I whisper thankfully.

And I wonder if this thing called life—if all that it really is, is a series of hand-holding episodes, a pulling of one another up out of the seemingly impossible to the experience of the possible.

I stand by the sign, victory fist in the air, as Harold takes my photo.

~~~~~~~~

Isaac Newton's pearls of gravitational wisdom whisper in my head. "What goes up must come down."

But I am saving all my thanks for second-in-command John.

That uphill terrain of scree is an equally maddening surface to descend.

Gravity grabs us and makes our strides swift, using an entirely different set of muscles and putting my knees through joint boot camp. The slippery scree makes balancing an issue and within the first twenty minutes, I fall on my butt, topple like a drunkard, and roll.

John, identical to Harold's gesture upon ascension, grabs my hand. We are off, accelerating like tandem skiers, using a heel-toe rapid-fire walk that requires equal parts balance and mobility. It is rough on both knees and shins but I say a quick prayer of gratitude for my trainer Philippe back in Atlanta who made those mobility exercises our number one priority the past year.

In less than an hour we are back on solid terrain.

The entire descent to the bottom of the national park takes a day and a half. We sleep at Millenium Camp after having traveled down to Barafu, gathering remains from the night before and continuing on for another two hours. In total, that final summit day plus our beginning descent is around 13 hours.

Millenium Camp is beautiful, or is it the relief within me that makes it so?

It doesn't take much for any of us to collapse and sleep that evening.

The next morning, our last delivery of ginger tea arrives and tastes extra satisfying.

Drinking it, I stare off into the distance as the bright sun casts its rays off Mount Meru. The porters gather around us and we are serenaded by a song, a long-held tradition on the final day of the Kilimanjaro adventure.

A few more hours and we will be back to the tropical rainforest area and then, finally, the final registration booth and state park exit where we will receive our official certificate for mastering the illustrious mountain.

My mind wanders to a scripture from the book of Malachi in the Biblical text that contains the words *prove me now*. The word *prove* is, I've come to believe, the great impetus for this entire adventure. How can I *prove* philosophical principles that I profess to believe in, that I've built my whole life around, unless I do so through action?

I continue the descent feeling the unparalleled satisfaction and quiet, internal joy that was birthed from such an action. I now have a greater depth of experience for having applied the *prove me now* energy as an intention. In these last hours, I feel physically capable of more than I could imagine, expect, or hope for. All of us are.

Now to maintain that sense of invincibility in the everyday world.

1) Do you ever feel it valuable to examine the things you feel you cannot do? Not things you do not want to do but things you are *intrigued* by yet somehow feel inherently incapable of doing? What are some of those things?

2) What reasons have you told yourself that make these intriguing dreams seem impossible? In all honesty, are they impossible? If not, then what is the resistance?

3) The referenced sacred scripture from the book of Malachi contains the phrase *prove me now*. It is a personal invitation for each of us to un-cover just how capable we are to powerfully live out our unlimited natures in a world that appears to be limited. What action is calling you to prove that infinite nature in your own life?

4) Harold is a real flesh-and-blood archetype of the protector—an embodiment of care, stead-fastness, wisdom, patience, and loving persis-tence. Have there been Harolds in your life? Have you allowed yourself to trust, surrender, and be absorbed in their caregiving or has fear distanced you from those opportunities?

You Have Options

> You can never have a happy ending at the end of an
> unhappy journey; it just doesn't work out that way.
> The way you're feeling, along the way, is the way
> you're continuing to pre-pave your journey, and it's
> the way it's going to continue to turn out until you
> do something about how you're feeling.
>
> – Abraham-Hicks

There's a fairly common workshop exercise designed to
shine light on the idea that we do not travel this life path
alone. I've always referred to it as an *affiliation circle*.

After discerning the exercise's appropriateness, given
the dynamics of the group, I have folks stand in one large
circle.

Starting off jovial and light, I'll ask, "How many have
had coffee this morning?" Those who have are asked to step
into the center of the circle, acknowledge their counterparts
through eye contact, then step back into the circumference
of the original circle.

Next, it might be a question like, "How many have traveled more than 100 miles to be here?" Again, those who have step into the middle of the larger circle, acknowledge with eye contact the others who have also stepped in, then move back into the original circle.

I then begin exploring deeper, more personal and emotional terrain.

"How many of you are working more than one job to make ends meet?

"How many of you are experiencing a foreclosure or the dissolution of a marriage or significant relationship?

"How many of you have family members who are battling some form of addiction? How many of you are currently involved in a recovery program of your own?"

We explore even deeper.

"How many of you were raised in a hostile environment where you suffered sexual abuse, incest, or rape?"

Each time, willing participants who have experienced these things step into the circle, acknowledge the others who have bravely entered with them, and then step back into the original circle.

Inevitably someone will ask, "What's the point? Why bring all of this up?"

As I mentioned in the beginning, the point is to bust the myth that we are alone in our circumstances, alone in our sorrows, and alone in our personal shame. We all travel this life path together and there are many who share our same story.

Yet I feel there's an even greater, deeper reasoning behind the exercise and that is to understand that our personal pain . . .

. . . isn't special.

Making our pain special is much like living our lives in waist-deep quicksand, never fully sinking yet never fully moving.

My father died when I was seven and afterwards I was regularly beaten and screamed at by a rage-aholic mother who simply mimicked the despair she had experienced as a child. I was barely average in the world of academia and failed miserably in my early attempts to find my place in the world. Based on religious beliefs, my discoveries and desire for love and intimacy were fueled by the shame of being a homosexual. This was followed by relationship after relationship where I was going to "help" my partners discover how great life could be—really nothing more than ego at play so I could avoid reconciling my own shit. Nearly all those relationships ended badly and my emotional heart felt like a broken mosaic glued together with a recurring history of shimmering mistakes.

In the mid-1980s, my beginnings towards embracing a more conscious, fulfilled life led me to study A Course in Miracles. It was there I first came across the concept of "special relationship"—that false allure that convinces us that someone else will complete us and fill the void of emptiness we may be experiencing. Those relationships, the course teaches, are destructive, selfish, and childishly egocentric. Yet once we become aware of looking outside ourselves for fulfillment, those relationships can transform into lessons of deep empowerment and personal forgiveness and become our holiest relationships because of the immense elevation in awareness that we gain.

I certainly had a vast collection of "special" relationships with the people in my life—those whom I thought might be able to fix or complete my perceptions of personal brokenness. But I also reflected on how any of us can create a special relationship with stories of drama and pain as well. The deeper question we might ask is, "Who would I be without my pain?"

By creating our own brand of specialness around the tragic divorce, the betrayal and abandonment, the demonizing of another person or institution, the loss of whomever, the layoff, the failed business, the dysfunctional parent, the burned down house, the disease, then *specialness* becomes the ringmaster with the bullwhip and we are nothing more than the controlled animal inside the ring.

We become more invested in honoring our labels of tragedy than we do in moving forward and getting on with the business of living.

Again, if you find this viewpoint angering, please understand that none of this is about discrediting your journey and what you have gone through to get where you are today. But consider that your current life is served either by looking ahead and using the collective wisdom from your journey to make wiser decisions or by looking back and continually beating the dead horse of your past.

Thankfully, I have never stopped my own personal search for a deeper understanding for why I am here and what it is I am to do. I'm grateful and humbled that over time, I woke up to the simple awareness that by holding on to the "specialness" of my pain—my story—nothing would ever change.

Consider this:

When we subscribe to the belief that the story of our pain is "special"—that our circumstances are somehow so far removed from anyone else's experience, so beyond anyone else's ability to understand—then we completely shut ourselves off from experiencing the freedom from that pain, freedom we say we want, freedom that many pay good money to therapists, psychiatrists, and counselors to learn how to achieve.

Could it be that a swifter path towards measurable, personal freedom comes from remembering this one simple thing: in this present moment you have options?

I believe we have options about every single facet of our earthly lives. Options on how to react, how to perceive, how to feel, where to go, whom to go with. Most importantly, we have options on how to think.

We have options on how long and to what degree we will dwell in the memories and the energies of a personal injustice or whether we will set our sights on what is available for us now.

We have options on whether we take ownership of our feelings or hold others hostage by believing that they are responsible.

My late father had an older sister named Willie Mae. As a young girl, Willie Mae was physically lanky, intro-verted, and awkward in both stature and social graces. But at seventeen, she crossed paths with a mid-twenties character named Sid who had befriended her tribe of brothers. Sid was suddenly a constant around the family house. He drank, smoked, played guitar, and talked of travel which branded him mysterious and seemingly unscathed by depression-era circumstances. He drove a well-worn Kissel. He was hardly considered respectable by my grandparents but my uncles were mesmerized by his nonconformity and so was Willie Mae. Family legend said it happened fast. One day they were both gone. Willie Mae left with Sid. Not a word from either of them. Less than a month later she was back. They had quickly wed and he, weeks later, quickly left. No one ever knew all the circumstances but she kept his last name and waited for him to return. She waited all the way up till her death at the age of 79. "He ruined her," the family often whispered. She was like a reincarnated Miss Havisham from Dicken's *Great Expectations*, living out her life in humiliation.

When I met her, as a little boy, she was wildly eccentric and mostly mean-spirited. She would often call my mother, accusing my older brothers of stealing from her. Minister and author Will Bowen once wrote that hurt people hurt people. That was an accurate assessment for my Aunt Willie Mae. Her world was one of accusations and threats. Hurt people hurt people and we are called upon to break the cycle rather than regenerate more of the same.

Author Byron Katie wrote, "As long as you think the cause of your problem is 'out there'—as long as you think that anyone or anything is responsible for your suffering—the situation is hopeless. It means that you are forever in the role of victim, that you're suffering in paradise."

And what amplifies that suffering so often is that we *pretend* that we don't have options, that we are helpless or powerless to forces outside us.

This may have been your reality before you reawakened from your deep sleep but it is not your reality anymore.

This pretending that we are bound, we believe, will somehow cushion our pain, but it actually prolongs it, intensifies it, and makes life unbearable at best.

You have options. I have options. Therefore, we can choose to thrive and experience genuine happiness in this world, or we can choose to withhold our joy because of retaliation, prejudice, resentment, grievance, or self-loathing.

If you are reading this, then I strongly believe something within you is ready to examine your relationship with prolonged pain. You are reading this by choice, not chance, and by continuing this long with the narrative then perhaps something is being stirred up and ready to be looked at. It can be immensely uncomfortable to excavate old patterns of blame or to stop telling the juicy story of how you were done wrong. But being uncomfortable is good. In fact, it is necessary for any substantial growth. We are powerfully reminded in the often-referenced quote from the 12-step tradition that pain is inevitable, yet the prolonged suffering from that pain is optional.

Imagine what Willie Mae's life might have been had she stood in an affiliation circle and discovered that she was not the only one who had ever been abandoned. Imagine the untold ways she could have processed and moved through her pain and come out the wiser.

I, too, imagine how much happier my own mother would have been had she met other struggling mothers whose husbands also died, leaving them with children to feed and a home to manage. How she could have channeled that fear, helplessness, and anger and moved on towards something empowering, welcoming talents and resilience that were left uncovered.

I know this is not easy. Making our past pain special is very seductive. If we never liberate ourselves from our victim status we will gravitate to others who share our "ain't it awful" sensibility and continue to argue favorably for our pain. It takes little effort to recruit others to support us in keeping the aura of *special* polished and shiny.

I've watched in awe the various interviews by Francine and David Wheeler whose six-year-old son Benjamin was killed in the Sandy Hooks Elementary School shooting on December 14, 2012 in Newtown, Connecticut. Many of us may never know the depth of their personal feelings of loss and anger nor the process that both parents went through in the privacy of their emotional journey. But what is evident is that there was a process, a very conscious, deliberate process that culminated in both of them sharing how their main objective from this day forward was to be an advocate for love. Addressing the United States gun control laws are obviously of vital importance to them, yet their main path of individual and collective healing is to learn how to love more. Perhaps what makes these parents stand out in a journalistic landscape accustomed to shining its focus on sensationalistic emotion is their allegiance to hope. Francine Wheeler so eloquently shared, "You can never fill that hole in your heart, but what you can do is cover your heart with all of this love so that your heart becomes bigger than the hole. Love can only grow and our job is to make our hearts bigger than the loss."

They do not deny that there was or is immense pain, yet they speak of the lessons learned, the vision and mission they see before them, and how to continue to be parents to Benjamin even though his physical body is no longer here.

Where to Start

If the willingness is there, I suggest you begin examining and acknowledging your current stories of pain, the degree of your attachments to how you've made any of it sacrosanct, and then determine whether you are ready to walk down that road of dissolution.

I would continue with a gentle approach of not trying to fix anything. Simply be aware that you feel hurt. Do not attach a person or situation to the pain. Simply acknowledge it. For example, instead of saying, "They hurt me," try saying, "I hurt." Period.

Relinquishing responsibility for the painful experience, followed by a willingness to simply acknowledge the feeling, frees the feeling from its historical importance and lessens its cherished place of residency inside us.

It does not mean that hurt will not revisit us again. It does not mean that we will be devoid of pain. But much like the ebb and flow of the ocean's tide, it can now come and, most importantly, go like any other feeling and experience. We simply honor it without resistance or judgment much

113

like we would with happiness, disappointment, elation, or remorse. If we subscribe to a belief that everything is connected, that there is a Universal All—a part of an Infinite Intelligence, Source, God, whatever you choose to call It—then doesn't the vast array of human emotion also exist in that Allness?

Next, consider that all that unprocessed, pent up pain is much like a ball of stagnant energy that sits within us, leaking out into our internal organs and interactive systems, eroding our well-being. Einstein claimed that "energy cannot be created or destroyed, it can only be changed from one form to another." The holding on of unprocessed pain is the same as holding on to stagnant energy, creating blockage and interrupting the system's ability to work in harmony with one another. We cannot destroy that energy but we can direct its exit out of our bodies through conscious integrative breathwork and physical activity. One can also visualize the energy and "scream it out." This is not screaming at another but finding a safe place, like the inside of a car, and screaming from your diaphragm, all the while visualizing that old stagnant energy leaving your body through the mouth.

Many years ago, I felt abandoned by someone who had left our relationship in addition to our mutually shared, mutually agreed upon financial responsibilities. That abandonment festered into an unprecedented rage. If you were willing to listen, I was willing to share how wretched and irresponsible I felt that behavior was. Yet unprocessed rage was incongruent with my life path as a minister and I was just as much out of integrity by not doing anything about it as I was of denouncing the other person.

I could feel that abandonment like a ball in the pit of my stomach. So I began to scream. I lived 17 minutes from where I was serving as a senior minister and every day as I got in the car and drove to work, I screamed. It was not at anyone, it was a deliberate conscious expulsion of that ball of energy that oddly enough became my spiritual practice. I screamed on the way to work and I screamed on the way home. I would often stop at the edge of my driveway in the evening to see if I could feel any shifts. There were nights when I could feel a palpable shift, a tangible resolve. There were many others where just the thought of the situation would stir the emotional pot and I would back the car out and continue driving and screaming some more. Other nights I simply said, "I'll pick this back up in the morning."

For three months I screamed. Towards the end of that 90-day experiment, I went for a walk with my two golden retrievers. It was a clear night and as I let them off their leashes to run in an adjacent field by my home, I paused and looked up at the dark sky. Stars blinked back at me and I became transfixed at how close they seemed. I wondered if the rest of the world was paying attention to the sky above them. In that moment, the thought of this person entered into my awareness and for the first time in over a year, the rage and animosity were gone. I felt a genuine desire for him to find peace in his life and hoped he was doing well.

All became quiet. And, without great fanfare or emotion, I simply knew that I had finally experienced true forgiveness. That unorthodox spiritual practice had emptied out whatever emotions I had blocked by judging him as inappropriate and unholy. I had poured out the bucket of pain.

The next day I received a phone call from that person offering an apology for all that had happened. It was lovely to receive, yet the best part was I no longer needed it.

Lastly, practice acceptance. Accept that there were certain life situations that were, for all intents and purposes, awful and messy. Accept that, but don't let any of it define you. Understand that every encounter on our personal timeline has been accompanied by the persistent energy of change. Perhaps we were too afraid, too unskilled to know how to properly invite change in. Hindsight develops maturity and we learn not to resist or fear change but to accept it. This act of acceptance does not make us weak. It reveals we are wise.

Albert Camus said, "Life is the sum of all your choices." There are still choices to be made and there is still much of your life yet to be formed. You have options.

1) How did the phrase "your pain isn't special" make you feel?

2) Are there painful circumstances that you have processed and successfully dissolved? What were the insights that came to you after that?

3) Are there ones you feel are too crucial to your personal story to simply let go?

4) Are there feelings you have labeled as appropriate and inappropriate? If so, what feelings do you judge? Are you willing to consider that every feeling has value?

5) Are there some things you feel are unforgiveable? If so, how does sustaining the energy of that affect you physically?

6) De-personalizing the pain, integrated breathwork/physical action (e.g., screaming), and acceptance are valuable tools to move through the paralysis of pain. Have you encountered other practices that were helpful?

Shut the Hell Up

> Truth walks toward us on the paths of our questions. As soon as you think you have the answer, you have closed the path and may miss vital new information. Wait awhile in the stillness and do not rush to conclusions no matter how uncomfortable the unknowing. Stay with the question.
>
> – Jacqueline Winspear

Maneuvering through the crowd, my partner and I marveled at getting a firsthand look at the magnificent paintings and sculpture that, prior to our Paris travels, had only been experienced through photographs. We were thrilled to be inside the Louvre, the world's most visited museum, and we felt rather travel savvy, having avoided the larger crowds by booking an early evening tour online. Yet, even with this reservation, there still were lingering waves of patrons throughout the massive structure vying for photo opportunities of the Venus de Milo and Winged Victory. The largest congestion of bodies was in the section that housed Leonardo da Vinci's iconic portrait known round

119

the world as the Mona Lisa. People pushed and elbowed their way closer to the freestanding wall where the famous painting hangs and divides the gallery. I noticed that the overwhelming majority of the visitors packed in this area were either oblivious to or purposefully ignoring the dozens of other paintings displayed to the front, back, left, and right of Mona's smirk of a smile. Like metal to magnet, they seemed irresistibly drawn to the 30- by 20-inch image preserved behind glass, feverishly snapping photographs and attempted selfies with their phones and cameras.

Standing and observing it all, the relentless inquirer within me wanted to know why. Why the Mona Lisa? And in the words of Wikipedia, why was she "the best known, the most visited, the most written about, the most sung about, the most parodied work of art in the world."

There are many speculations among critics that make substantive guesses to try and answer these questions regarding Da Vinci's work, but the reality is no one really knows. No one can authentically track all of the data, offer a complete list of names, give definitive timelines, or offer reliable facts. It's all guesswork and centuries' worth of conjecture.

There have been many times throughout my life where this same inner inquirer was stirred and awakened from its conformist napping.

And like the incessant questioning of an adolescent, I've often wanted to know why things are the way they are. My curiosity was not so much geared towards the geological as it was the sociological.

For example, before I even fully comprehended what an abolitionist or suffragist was, I wanted to know why some people were looked down upon while others were favored. Why did we not love thy neighbor as ourselves—a mainstay of the ten commandments and the golden rule that I had dutifully memorized?

My inner inquirer generated regular upset in Sunday School class at First Assembly of God in Beaumont, Texas.

I wanted to know why Abraham's wife, Sarah, could have a child at 90 years of age after my oldest sister informed me that older women couldn't make babies anymore.

I wanted to know why we should get haircuts if Samson lost his strength because of getting one.

I wanted to know why Jonah was the only documented person to survive inside the belly of a whale for three days and how he did that without air, food, or water.

I wanted in-depth explanations of every biblical story and an answer for why these circumstances and perceived miracles were not relatable to the world around me.

The one answer consistently given was that a Christian simply had to believe—believe without question for it is written in the Bible and the Bible is the infallible word of God.

If I ever strayed beyond the permissive lines of what was deemed acceptable I was swiftly reprimanded.

Yet to question everything is not only healthy, it is an inherent part of human behavior. Curiosity, the wonder behind the why, drives our seeking natures to take action. It is the only thing that can effectively scratch the itch of our perpetual longings. Socrates taught that wonder is the beginning of wisdom. Perhaps that is why we are encouraged by the wise to never lose our sense of childlike wonder. Why is the word wonder so often preceded by the adjective "childlike"?

Some sort of demarcation line seems to exist for most of us. We stop our healthy questioning and blindly accept what is presented without checking inward to see how the information even feels. Perhaps it is the collateral damage of adulthood and the building up of comparison and cynicism beautifully absent in our adolescence that makes us stop exploring the why behind it all. Such blind acceptance does, in lazy displays of personal growth, free us from the responsibility of having to think for ourselves. We become the one who allows the words "because I said so, that's why!" to be the mantra we live by.

Like millions of others, I was raised in a household where the religion of choice was pro-hell as an afterlife destination. This hell, we are taught, is a place our souls will be sentenced to if we do not abide by the Judeo-Christian ethics outlined for salvation. This hell becomes the single most powerful thing we fear. Subsequently, it influences the trajectory of our lives' behavioral choices and beliefs. Every act of an individual can be judged as moral and upright or vile and depraved. Whatever way our choices gravitate determines our reservation in the afterlife. The fault of any depravity and pain is due to the temptations of Satan, the nemesis of God, whose only mission is to rob you and me of our spots in Heaven and claim us as residents of his eternal fire.

The fear of hell, then, becomes our moral compass and our flawed human enactments require a constant repentance of sin—the repeated practice one must do to get back into the good graces of a scorekeeping God who judges our every move.

As I reflect back on all the events that led to questioning this literal concept of hell, there lives a profound sense of gratitude and empowerment for the courage to do so. The willingness to consider the possibility of something different, to allow my inner inquirer to even dare question something so magnanimous as hell, then to ultimately change my belief, was a life changer.

The undercurrent of my divine discontent that formed as a teenager began to find relief in a shared dressing room with a fellow actor in Bucks County, Pennsylvania. On our joined countertop among stage makeup and props was a copy of the book *Out on a Limb* by Shirley MacLaine. When he relayed that the book was about her out-of-the-box spiritual explorations, I remember automatically shutting down, a reflex reaction fueled by some ingrained condemnation regarding its controversial content. The irony was that even though I had stopped going to church, the doctrine of church was still "going" in me. He explained his beginning fascination in esoteric philosophical concepts and that he found validation for what he was feeling in MacLaine's writing. I muttered something to the effect of "not interested," even though years before I had professed my own disillusionment in the dogma of my religious upbringing.

He was exploring other philosophical ideas and I was in conformist limbo. He was looking beyond the Mona Lisa and I was still stagnating on the periphery of the common crowd, not really invested but not even aware there were other places to look.

Nonetheless, I could not get my dressing room mate's words out of my head and when our summer season of shows was complete, I bought the book at the train station, immediately devouring MacLaine's spiritual tour-de-force as I rode back into Manhattan. For the next few days I read and reread it from cover to cover.

What leapt off the pages for me were the references regarding the Council of Nicea, Emperor Justinian, his irrepressible and power hungry wife, Empress Theodora, the Nicene Creed, and the hypothesis that hell was a concept introduced into scripture by these collective religious leaders as a way to instill control over the masses.

I remember my heart pounding in my chest like a tribal drum, shouting at me to wake up and return to my long forgotten home. Within those pages I felt as though I had stumbled upon the answer to my biggest why.

Why would God destroy mankind, something made in His own likeness and image, by sending it to an everlasting experience of torture due to transgressions when we were also taught to forgive one another seventy times seven, a metaphor for forgiving constantly? Why would some people go to hell simply because of geography? How did I, as an American Christian, win the religion lottery when others born in countries practicing a faith different than my own lose out?

Thus began a quest for deeper ecclesiastical studies, linguistics, and cultural connotations. I had to acknowledge the spiritual arrogance I had inherited. I uncovered that the word "hell" did not exist in first century Israel and was not even used until approximately AD 725. Its origin is not Hebrew and, according to *The Barnhart Concise Dictionary of Etymology*, the word "hell" was adopted into our vocabulary as a way to introduce the pagan concept of hell into Christian theology—which it did quite successfully. Christian historians, such as Benjamin Corey, Kurt Willems, and many more, reveal that the word hell uttered by Jesus in biblical scripture was the translation for the word Hinnom, a valley outside the gates of Jerusalem where garbage and dead bodies were often discarded and consumed by fire that likely burned continuously. It was a literal reference to a place that was highly undesirable. It was not some underworld. It was referenced repeatedly as an indication of somewhere to avoid, much like our modern slang has taken the word gutter (a conduit for filthy waste) and now uses that word to describe a location of vulgarity and sordidness where our thoughts go or a place that describes our rock-bottom emotional low point.

Hell for Christian progressives, metaphysicians, humanists, freethinkers, and those aligned with inclusive paths for personal devotion use it to describe a state of consciousness just as its counterpart heaven is used. I can live in heaven now—heaven on earth—by the deliberate transformation of my thoughts from lack, jealousy, and self-degradation to ones of love, forgiveness, gratitude, and kindness. That is heaven consciousness. And I am free to live in the hell of my own making, viewing the world as depleted, unfair, futile, unsafe, and fueled by an us-versus-them mentality. That is hell consciousness.

The celebrated author and Christian apologist C.S. Lewis famously wrote this regarding hell. "Hell is a state of mind—ye never said a truer word. And every state of mind, left to itself, every shutting up of the creature within the dungeon of its own mind—is, in the end, Hell. But Heaven is not a state of mind. Heaven is reality itself. All that is fully real is Heavenly. For all that can be shaken will be shaken and only the unshakeable remains."

As a little boy I remember being wildly excited about attending a Vacation Bible School held in a neighborhood Baptist church. There were cookies and punch, arts and crafts, storytelling—things that were still special events in my world. In the art portion of the week-long event, all the children were busy designing their own picture books on the Life of Jesus, illustrating famous stories of him on thick paper then finally binding each picture together with twine. In every drawing of mine, whether it was turning the water into wine, raising Lazarus from the dead, even the crucifixion, I drew Jesus with flowing blonde hair. When the teacher asked me about his hair color, I replied, "Because blondes have more fun," mimicking a popular hair coloring product commercial tagline of the time. In my childlike world view, Jesus always seemed so sad and put upon, continuously helping so many people only to later be betrayed. I felt bad for him and my automatic impulse was to find a way to help. Blonde locks seemed the best way to offer him support.

The teacher was not amused and I was reprimanded for mocking the Savior and sent home with my blasphemous illustrations. I was too dumbfounded and embarrassed to ask why I was being sent home, but when I shared my picture book with my dad and told him what happened, he simply smiled and replied, "Some folk are just allergic to being happy." He told me, in his Texas drawl, he thought Jesus looked "right nice with blonde hair." His response is one of the few treasured conversations I remember having with my dad before his death.

Being sent home accompanied by the development of shame was hell. My dad's reaction was heaven.

Themes

If heaven and hell are "states of mind" or the reflection of one's perception of the outside world, then how did these perceptions come to be?

The twentieth century American philosopher Ernest Holmes wrote that when we understand the use of Spiritual Law, a law that teaches the reciprocal nature of creation—that it is done unto us as we believe—then we are where we are because of what we are. The "what we are" component is made up of our state of mind. The beauty of transformation from any limitation is that you and I do not need to know the specifics of the origin of past beliefs in order to create a new state of mind. However, I have found that it is helpful to recognize the recurring themes in our behaviors and lifestyle choices throughout the course of our lives.

A popular theme is "if I want something done right I need to do it myself." That theme, I confess, is one that I subconsciously lived my life from for many years. It doesn't matter where it actually began, but perceiving that as a truth produced, by spiritual law, a current example of modern day hell. Having that theme meant that all that could show up for me regarding support had to match that theme. Every theme has its mental equivalents. It cannot be anything above that perception because that was all that I was allowing myself to perceive. How did that play out? Regular episodes of "flawed" people showing up, mismanagement, personality conflicts, even betrayal. These predictable equivalents are in alignment with embracing such a theme.

If you dissect this theme of having to do it all, you will find that it is rooted in the need to maintain control. When you dissect that theme, you will find there is a fear of making mistakes. When you dissect that theme, you will find a fear of being judged, and when you dissect that theme you will find a fear of not being enough. At my core I felt I was not enough and what showed up for me was a reflection of what I thought about myself.

This state of mind, or hell perception, perpetuates itself until there is a moment of clarity that speaks to your authentic self and suggests that this perception does not have to remain.

As Ernest Holmes powerfully stated, "Change your thinking, change your life."

Some of the other common themes I see among those I counsel are:

- As a single parent I am the sole person respon-sible.

- There isn't enough time.

- I am too old, too young, too thin, too fat.

- I will always be in debt.

- There is too much competition.

- Once they get to know the real me, then they are gone.

These themes, once dissected—once the smoke-screen excuses are removed—lead us to the universal root of unworthiness.

Shut the Hell Up

So if you are willing to consider the premise that hell is a choice, a state of mind, then how do you begin to redirect your thoughts towards its alternative? The only answer I find legitimate to any question such as this is through one's own sense of awareness. When noticing any mental "hell" activity, one of the healthiest things we can do is to acknowledge its existence.

- I am engaged in an argument in my head with someone who isn't even here.

- I am noticing that I'm self-critical about my looks.

- I am noticing that I just deflected a compliment.

- I am noticing that I have a theme going on about having to do everything myself if I want something done right.

The act of noticing these thoughts as they are happening is your sweet spot to transformation. It is these priceless moments of awareness that allow you to shut the "hell" up and start course correcting your deliberate mental focus towards something more heavenly. You can gently reply to yourself, "Ah, look at that. I'm repeating an old pattern that actually has no valid reality. Is this worth sacrificing my heaven on earth?" If, from one moment of awareness to the next, you turn the mental focus around to a greater idea—a heavenly reality about all the things that are working rather than what are not—then opportunities that already exist in our world can finally have space within you to reside. We call this our spiritual practice but I believe it has the opportunity to be even more than that—it can become our lifestyle.

A few years back I journeyed by bus through the Czech countryside from Prague to a quaint spa town called Karlovy Vary. I made eye contact with a restless young boy of about five or six who sat in the row ahead of me. He was obviously uncomfortable, bouncing in his seat, turning around, popping his head up and down above the top of the headrest while trying to gain attention from those of us behind him.

I gave in and started reciprocating with my own version of peek-a-boo. As he looked over the seat, I'd hide my face in my hands. As he ducked down, I'd remove them. He'd peek through the cracks between the seat during his hiding phase and see my hands down. He would then bounce back up and I'd hide my face again. Back and forth we would go and I was sure he would tire of this game sooner than later. I underestimated his stamina. For the entire two-hour bus ride, he proved to be an insatiable peek-a-boo addict. No matter how many times I stopped, reached down and pretended to get something out of my bag, opened a book, his bouncing continued undaunted.

Our journey with hell is much the same way. When we can't make the decision to remain honorable to ourselves then the world becomes disinterested or fatigued with us, much like I began feeling towards the boy on the bus. We might hide from some old buried pain by fashioning a pretense that we have it all together, yet it only resurfaces time and again in inappropriate ways. It's as if we are engaged in a relentless game of spiritual peek-a-boo.

> *I'm going to let out my magnificence/I'm going to take it back.*
> *I'm going to behave boldly/I'm going to shrink in fear.*
> *I can do it/I can't do it.*
> *I'm going to stand up for myself/I'm going to cave in and let others dominate me.*

Essentially it becomes:

> *I'm worthy/I'm not worthy.*
> *I'm worthy/I'm not worthy.*
> *I'm worthy/I'm not worthy,*
> *and on and on.*

Unworthiness is the hell of every man.

Choosing Heaven

The quote at the beginning of this chapter by mystery writer Jacqueline Winspear offers telling wisdom: "Truth walks toward us on the paths of our questions."

How beautiful and honoring to know that our innate sense of wondering why is part of the journey to experiencing answers to our personal questions.

To question leads to revelation. Revelation is part of the circular flow of energy that starts with the inception of thought, which, if allowed, travels to exploration and experience. Our experiences help formulate our authentic answers.

Notice I said *our* answers and not *the* answers.

Answers are never held in a one-size-fits-all container unless we are talking about the fundamental question regarding the meaning and reason for life—whatever the question, love is the answer. But if I have questions regarding where I should live, what career best matches my passions, and what lifestyle choices reflect my inner qualities, these answers, based on human conditioning and preferences, are as varied as the questions themselves.

Author Cristina Marrero said, "To question the world around us and all its complexities is not blasphemy, but simply using the mind God gave us for its intended purpose. God is an artist. Artists do not create to have someone just glance and say 'That is pretty.' Artists want viewers to look closer, deeper—to really see what they have created—not just glance."

I believe that sustaining heaven consciousness for as much as we can, for as long as we can, becomes our most sacred calling. To be able to question everything, yet paradoxically know that all things in the Universe self-regulate towards greater intelligence and greater love, is choosing to live life from the inside out. It's developing a mental prototype for what it is you long for and devotedly dwelling on its full possibility. Life is calling you to dive headfirst into the mystery. Be willing to learn from the messes and the victories. Refine your choices but don't make the past wrong. Continue on with unwavering hope and heart. That is the gift of life. That is heaven on earth.

1) What is your relationship with questioning the information you daily receive? How much of what you hear and read do you blindly accept? How would you describe your relationship with your inner inquirer—neglectful, casual acquaintance, or constant companion?

2) In what areas do you feel that questioning has served you? When do you feel it may have hindered you?

3) I refer to awareness as the sweet spot of transformation. Why is awareness so crucial to your conscious growth?

4) From personal reflection, do you see any recurring themes that characterize your life? If so, does this theme(s) serve you? If not, what new theme are you willing to start welcoming in?

5) What does heaven on earth mean to you? On a scale of 1–10 with 10 being the highest, how would you rate heaven's presence in your life?

Dying Many Deaths

> All walking is discovery. On foot we take the time
> to see things whole.
>
> — Hal Borland

I'd never thought much about the definition of the word
pilgrim. As a child born in the United States, I'd long ago
assumed that a pilgrim was the name solely granted to those
folk with the funny clothes who came over to America on
a boat called the Mayflower, the ones who celebrated by
cooking turkey and eating with Indians.

But those pilgrims who founded the colony of
Plymouth, Massachusetts were simply being added to an
endless list of others who already were and would continue
to define themselves by that name.

What is a pilgrim? By dictionary definition it is a person
who journeys a long distance to some sacred place as an act
of religious devotion.

I am now a pilgrim.

I earned that title by walking the ancient medieval trail
known as the Camino de Santiago from the latter part of

May to the beginning days of July in 2009, starting in the picturesque border town of Saint-Jean-Pied-de-Port in France, climbing the Roncesvalles Pass across the Pyrenees down to the Spanish Basque territory, then continuing on the 800-plus-kilometer trek across the entire northern rim of Spain.

All totaled, I walked, climbed, and stumbled my way through every mile leaving footprints on an estimated 300 villages, hamlets, towns, and cities with nothing more than minimal provisions strategically arranged in a backpack.

The Camino de Santiago was the route traveled by kings, queens, misfits and holy men, saints and sinners—by Charlemagne, Napoleon, Joan of Arc, Dante, Chaucer, Saint Frances of Assisi, and on and on. The path covered the territory where the Knights Templar and the Moors clashed over religious freedom, a road some say mimics the design of the Milky Way and possesses tremendous energetic forces called ley lines throughout its ancient design.

The Camino pilgrims' desired arrival is the city of Santiago de Compostela, one of the farthest points north of Spain and believed to be the burial place of the Apostle James. It was this area that the saint had grown fond of while traveling and sharing the teachings of Christ. After being summoned back to Jerusalem around AD 44, he was beheaded by Herod Agrippa for his beliefs and became the first martyred apostle. What happened afterwards is a vibrant mix of folklore and legend, yet it is legend alone that forms the basis of the Camino's famous beginnings. The most popular story is how Saint James's remains were smuggled across the seas by his devoted followers to this

Spanish territory which he'd grown to love. Traveling across the Galecian countryside, oxen struggled to pull his heavy sarcophagus until, exhausted, they all but collapsed in a field. It was there his devotees hollowed out a grave and buried their beloved. Later in the ninth century, a shepherd tending his flock witnessed a low-hanging star cascading a bright light onto this same field. After hearing the story of the strange illumination, the local priests suggested a hole be dug where the star had shone upon the earth. And it was there they found the apostle's remains some eight centuries after his initial burial. News spread throughout the land that bones, so closely connected to the life of Jesus the Christ, were among them. Ceremoniously, a church was built to house the remains of Saint James (Santiago) from the field of the star (compostela), now known as Santiago de Compostela.

I first became aware of the Camino de Santiago (The Way of Saint James) through the book *The Pilgrimage*, the travelogue of Brazilian writer Paolo Coelho's own mystical journey and spiritual awakening on this pilgrim's path. Later came actress Shirley MacLaine's tale *The Camino*, chronicling her very different yet equally fascinating personal epiphanies on the centuries' old journey. It was also the focal point for the emotionally stirring motion picture *The Way*, written and directed by Emilio Estevez and starring him and his father, actor Martin Sheen.

So why was I here? Everyone loves an epiphany or two and I thought that turning 50 on the trail would be the perfect setting to receive one. My pilgrimage was *not* birthed from some duty to religious doctrine. It was more a spiritual compulsion born from listening to and trusting the callings of a nomadic, wanderlust heart. I was not attached to the possible bird's-eye view of mysteries, vortexes, and energy fields that might create the end-all be-all mystical experience, the ones I had read with lush detail in Coelho's work. Rather, I stayed dedicated to my intent to walk the Camino because my passions are fueled by intentions designed around challenging perceived personal limitations and because the desire to go and walk it never grew stale. Year after year, the trail, with a sort of incessant whisper, faithfully beckoned me.

Restless and excited on that first night prior to starting, I stared out the window of the albergue (a pilgrim's refuge stop) and into the night sky. The moon was ablaze, as if amping up its wattage especially for me. I stared hypnotically at its undeniable power as it cast an inextinguishable light over the hills surrounding Saint-Jean-Pied-de-Port. Snores wafted from the bunk beds around me from a group of Frenchmen quite at ease with the primitive surroundings. I would soon come to learn how ear plugs would become my most valued possession. Two tiny bits of foam would save my sanity far more than beds and showers.

Try as I might, I was unable to sleep. Raw, excited nervousness rocketed through my body. I rolled from side to side on my tiny bunk bed mattress, feeling like a child waiting for that elusive Christmas morning.

Excitement turned to dread, however, when, but hours later, the stark incline and the novelty of walking with weighted gear—rucksack, sleeping bag, staff, provisions—culminated in instant exhaustion. Oddly, it felt less like physical exhaustion and more like an emotional draining following some relentless, seismic, mental rant that criticizes and shakes you at your core—"You're doing it all wrong. Everyone else seems fine." It was as though a wave of shame was pulling me down, suffocating me with such intensity that, at times, I would have welcomed physical death. How could I fail so fast?

"You should have trained more," I inwardly scolded.

And all along the way people kept passing.

Not just physically fit people, not just the stereotypical males with testosterone fueled motivation, but nearly everyone. Women—thin women, zaftig women, teens—and even the requisite herd of sheep all seemed to outpace me as we traversed through the unfamiliar landscape.

The game of mental comparison starting within my thoughts continued weakening my physical capabilities. A low-level panic brewed around the possibility that perhaps this long-awaited adventure might be far more than I bargained for. More shame. As each pilgrim passed alongside my left and my right, there built up within me a fear that all of the sleeping accommodations allotted for those of us on the trail would be taken. My turtle-paced speed and struggles would equate to a "no room in the inn" outcome.

Prior to the trip, a spiritual mentor shared with me an intuitive insight he felt about my upcoming trek.

"You will die many deaths," he said.

I assumed the referral of death was about the ubiquitous things we're always chanting about removing from our lives—death of an old idea, not being good enough, unworthiness, etc.

It was. I just didn't realize that the "deaths" would start within the first day.

Death to Comparison and Worry

Midway in the midst of the ascent, I paused, sweaty and panting, and did a panoramic glance of my surroundings.

Many have commented on how temperamental the Pyrenees can be. With its low-hanging cloud cover, its dense mist and fog, it can refuse to offer the viewer the full scope of its outlying vistas. But not this day. No, this day it was clear, a day where atmospheric transparency assists you in discerning images, movements, and design from countless miles away.

How could anyone be miserable standing among such perfection? Yet, ironically, I was.

Maybe it was on this mountain that author Irving Stone received his inspiration for his novel *The Agony and the Ecstasy*, for I was deeply challenged by the agony I felt in my physical being and the contradictory euphoria, even ecstasy, I experienced when appreciating the beauty around me.

And finally all that internal questioning began opening up a portal of awareness around my most basic human functioning—comparing myself to others and worrying about the future.

In my world of effect, there will always be someone smarter, prettier/handsomer, richer, braver, and more talented. And eventually I've learned that the gift of life isn't about any of that; it's about ceaselessly taking inventory of all the gifts I do possess and never abusing them through the waste of comparison.

Taking inventory of our behavior, our motivations, is an unavoidable process that dutifully beckons all of us. It was Bill W., the founder of Alcoholics Anonymous who wrote, "For the wise have always known that no one can make much of his life until self-searching has become a regular habit, until he is able to admit and accept what he finds, and until he patiently and persistently tries to correct what is wrong."

At some early point in our development we began observing that there are differences to all the others around us. Large, small, dark, light, tall, short, we took in this information and processed it the way our elders did. We began modeling our opinions to be in alignment with the opinions we were surrounded by.

I grew up in a fundamentalist Christian environment. Church services were three times a week. God was a bizarre mixture of love and punishment, a God of moods that could easily be triggered by my actions. I was taught that other religious beliefs were missing something or were a complete abomination. Those paths were not "the" path. This dogmatic saturation structured my earliest beliefs until a divine discontent began chipping away at all of it and I could no longer contain myself within an exclusionary box that revered some and reviled others. The greatest moment in this dismantling was a sincere willingness to be wrong—to actually be willing to disobey the God of my childhood and gamble with the possibility of an eternal hell in order to honor the profound restlessness and questioning within my heart and mind.

Being willing to refuse the accepted standards, conventions, and rules surrounding God opened me to an awareness of God as an all-inclusive, perpetuating energy of life and love permeating all things, including myself. My new understanding became "God as all, in all, through all." It was a deep sense of resolve that felt like a homecoming of the soul.

I grew up witnessing how the acquisition of money was hard. I grew up hearing how love between people of the same sex was an abomination. I grew up being told that job security was far more valuable than pursuing your passions. So many of these early dictates made their way into my comparative thoughts. I was repeatedly told through word and example that there was only so much to go around so get while the getting is good. I locked onto the idea that my level of success was dependent upon the impressions I made on others. Being well-mannered and conforming was prized over being an original.

To be passed on the mountain by so many other travelers meant that I might not have a place to stay at the end of the day's passage. Since this was my first day to climb, I had no previous experience of what to expect. With that as a concern, these people were not fellow pilgrims, they were bed stealers and I needed to beat them in order to secure provision for myself. It was all that primal, childhood programming wanting to have a new surge of life inside me.

The worry of what might happen robs us of imagining all that could work in our favor. Worry is, quite simply, the negative use of our imagination.

From my awareness of and willingness to honestly own what was happening to me, I made the conscious decision to let go of my comparisons, let go of my concerns regarding shelter at the end of the day, and focus on the present moment adventure and all the remarkable beauty around me.

It was at that moment of decision that the phrase Solution Already Exists came into my mind.

This simple phrase coaxed me into considering that whatever needs I would be facing in the mysterious hours ahead were already met. All I needed was to allow myself to relax, to stop worrying about what might happen and continue putting one foot in front of the other.

As simple as it reads now, in the moment it felt revolutionary. I thought of the controversial explorer Christopher Columbus and his oft given title Discoverer of America. As I walked I realized that there was a technicality in this title. Columbus did not "discover" America. The land mass known as America already existed. What Columbus did was honor an intention and get in a boat. Lamentable temperament aside, he took an action. He set sail.

Our supposed discoveries are no different. What we desire is already in existence. Let me repeat that. What we desire is *already* in existence. Our part is to take the action to go and meet its already existing nature. Ours is a voyage of "uncovery" traveling in full confidence of our findings. That right and perfect creative expression with a great salary already exists. That magnificent home in the desired location already exists. The relationship that offers fulfillment and honoring companionship already exists.

Your only requirement is to own that truth as if it were the most natural thing in the world. Relax about the unknown factors that have yet to materialize. Set sail with your intentions to stay the course towards your desire and be in alignment with your thoughts, words, and deeds. Your devotion will guide you to its already existent shore.

Located around the earliest kilometers of the ancient trail are receptacles for over-packed pilgrims to begin their "emptying." We all travel through life with baggage. We voluntarily carry burdens that weigh us down and drain joy from our collective days. Inside my rucksack were one too many changes of clothes, books I thought I'd read along the way, extra provisions for the unexpected. I began emptying much of the must-haves into these designated barrels to be recycled for others to enjoy.

I was reawakening to the simple truth that life is not a race. There is no finish line. Who cares if on ascending trails I have to move at a snail's pace? And as swiftly as I died to these habits, I was reborn, feeling more comfortable in my own skin than I ever had before.

There was a bed that first night and for all the other nights to come. There was food when food was needed and, amusingly, there was an ATM or two, even in the barest of villages when more euros were needed for provisions.

I began filling these long, consecutive days of walking with a conscious decision to be in conversation with comparison and worry, inviting their deaths to continue.

Death to Inadequacy

On the descent into Puente la Reina, a few days into the journey, I was joined by Emmanuelle, a young Frenchman with Jesus hair who seemed to want to talk. "Ah, USA," he said, and when I told him at that time I was living in the state of Alabama, there was an immediate recognition of that word by singing "Sweet Home Alabama." No more lyrics after that, just the three starting words of the chorus. It was to be a repeated response without fail from everyone from countless countries.

Emmanuelle continued asking simple questions in broken English as we passed the time towards the day's destination. Then with all seriousness, he asked why I did not speak another language. I had no effective reasoning and he made me *aware* how everyone I'd met—everyone—was making some attempt to converse with me in English but I was unable to return the courtesy. I felt inadequate. I realized I could stay in that energy and become intimidated by it or I could enroll him and all my future fellow pilgrims in teaching me phrases. I chose the latter and filled page after page in my diary with multilingual conversations. I could tell it meant something to the other pilgrims to hear me attempt to express my honor of them and their journey with a simple "Te honro amigo peregrine."

Death to Injustice

On my tenth day of walking I reached the robust town of Santo Domingo de la Calzada, where an ornate cathedral sits among the shops, restaurants, and businesses that make up the main square. As I wandered in, a choir was rehearsing for an upcoming mass. The acoustics were glorious and the sound of the organ and the voices pulsed through me and captivated my full attention. Yet throughout the musical measures I swore I could hear crowing. As I looked upwards behind me, there on the cathedral's back wall was a permanent nesting pen housing a rooster and a hen.

Tradition tells that sometime in the fifteenth century a married couple and their eighteen-year-old son stopped here to rest at an inn as they made their pilgrimage to Santiago. The girl at the inn where they stayed fell in love with the youth, but her feelings were rebuffed. Bent on revenge, she placed a silver goblet in his luggage, and when the family continued their journey, the girl reported him to the local authorities. Under the laws of the time, the punishment for robbery was death. The innocent young man was sentenced and hanged. When the grieving parents set out to leave again towards Santiago, they stopped to retrieve their child's body at the sight of the hanging for proper burial. Arriving, they found him alive, telling how the saints had saved him. When it was reported to the authorities that the boy lived, the Commissioner scornfully replied that the young man was about as alive as the roasted rooster and hen he was about to eat. At that moment, the rooster and hen leapt from the plate and began to crow.

Today a live rooster and hen are replaced every month in the high-standing niche in the cathedral, reminding all that the miracle of truth always prevails.

With the choir still rehearsing, I sat on a hardened pew in the cathedral of Santo Domingo and began recalling a half century's worth of injustices. Abuse, abandonment, failures, and lost dreams. What righteous anger might still be brewing in my mind? What unfulfilled expectations might I be blaming another for? How much of me reflected the actions of that dejected girl at the inn and how much of me was the innocent boy?

The familiar melody of *Soul of My Savior* vibrated throughout the church and I knew that the ultimate saving of *my* soul had to do with a willingness to forgive myself for holding on to a belief that others had harmed me without consent. I could spend another fifty years keeping the justification of others as separate or I could own the fact that we are all connected and that I am a contributor to whatever has happened or will happen to me. My breathing deepened as I made room in my lungs, my mind, and my heart for the power I was reclaiming. "It is done unto us as we believe." There is no injustice, only an ever faithful "outpicturing" of our inner world of thought.

Death to Wishing Things Were Different

There were fierce, cold headwinds on the last day of my fortieth decade. I was approximately 250 kilometers into the journey when a biting chill and flying dirt began to hit me in the face. I calculated I had close to three more hours of walking to reach my destination of the village of Belorado. At times I felt the wind's force would knock me over. "This will stop soon," I reasoned, but it was not to be.

For those hours, I wrestled against the wind. I took a pair of socks and put them over my hands and layered on one more shirt. I now understood why people had lightweight jackets with them, though in the beginning of the pilgrimage it had seemed absurd. The wind chill was brutal.

Sunglasses shielded my eyes from the swirling dirt clouds and I pressed forward as best I could.

What was I doing in this seemingly impossible wind? Well, for one thing, I was letting it control me in every emotional and physical way. How could I let go of resisting it and allow the wind to just do its thing? I didn´t want this, not today. Not on the last day of my forties where I planned to walk in gratitude and examination of all the wondrous gifts life had delivered to me. This wind was spoiling my plans. While shivering, I channeled some inner crazy man and shouted to the wind.

"I *know* you are serving a purpose, and for that I thank you, but can you cooperate a little here?" It didn't listen. I tried thinking of all the gifts that wind brings like energy, propulsion, offering assistance to sailboats on water. Being angry at the wind was about as useful as being angry at summer changing into autumn. And finally, worn down by my judgment and resistance to what was, the shift in consciousness began to quietly work. Not that the wind stopped, mind you, but my obsession about it did. I visited my original intention to give thanks for my fortieth decade. Reflecting back on all the immense change and growth that had occurred during those ten years, it suddenly felt divinely inspired to be walking into these winds. They were clearing away any and all residue of limiting beliefs. I was to reach the milestone of 50 having my body, mind, and soul exfoliated by Mother Nature. With my mind on gratitude rather than the wind, those hours seemed to rapidly disappear. I entered the door of the village's pilgrim refuge feeling primed and readied for the next half century of adventure.

Death to Others' Approval

Upon arriving in the town of Hospital de Órbigo, I crossed what was to be the most famous of all bridges that pilgrims cross on this traditional route. It was a long, beautifully crafted, multi-arched stone structure dating back to the 11th century. It was written that Cervantes gained inspiration for his character Don Quixote here. On this very bridge a young knight opted to place a shackle around his neck and not remove it until he had defeated 300 of the country's finest swordsmen. His point: to prove to a maiden in this town his devotion and love for her. What an attention-getter. You wonder with all that turmoil and spent energy, the shackle, the amount of time it must have taken to knock off a total of 300 other knights, if she would have been as equally impressed by simply inviting her out for a moonlight walk and offering her a bouquet of hand-picked wildflowers.

I stopped to sit at the end of the bridge that connected to the town's main road and rest my back against the ancient stone. What if Cervantes had sat on this very spot and had the same realization? His masterpiece, *The Ingenious Gentleman Don Quixote of La Mancha*, weaves the tale of the nobleman Alonso whose mild madness sends him on a futile quest of fighting imaginary enemies. Likewise, there is a madness in fighting for external acceptance. Looking back down the length of this memorable bridge I wondered if the battle-prone knight of this village ever discovered the same?

I thought of all the times I'd operated just as the knight had throughout my life. I once believed that by working harder, stronger, faster, I would hopefully be noticed. Yet I was realizing that the effort never appeases the craving to be approved, accepted, or seen. I was completely clear that the degree I accepted and valued myself was the only degree I could expect that from another.

Death to Complaining

I felt a hunch to detour off the main path on the day's destination to the quaint town of Villafranca del Bierzo, more than six hundred kilometers from where I had begun the pilgrimage. I quickly scolded myself after realizing that I had picked a far more steep and rugged terrain than the easy common route along an asphalt highway. Yet later that day, the detour proved magical as it led me towards the back of Villafranca, bringing me directly to the Saint James Church and the infamous Doorway of Forgiveness. This was the Romanesque doorway built in the 12th century where, for centuries after, pilgrims who were too ill to continue the journey to Santiago passed through here and were granted an indulgence.

I walked up to its historic archway and became overcome with a profound sense of empathy and sorrow for what must have been one continuous experience of loss and heartbreak for the countless souls that would not reach Santiago. I reflected upon my petty aches and pains compared with the intense physical challenges so many of the medieval pilgrims endured—freezing temperatures, hunger, and hardships. Here is where they collapsed in their disappointment at not being able to continue the journey and where they were lovingly offered care and absolution. Perspective is the wisest of teachers, insistent on moving us from the jargonistic count-our-blessings stage of kindergarten gratitude to a deeper realization of life's inherent grace and goodness. Kneeling, I placed my head on the ancient door and forgave myself for the innumerable times I had taken for granted the precious and potent gift of life.

Death to Limitation and Conformity

Entering Santiago de Compostela, an odd sense of melancholy flooded my heart, knowing that the end of a long-held dream was coming to an end. I wanted those final steps to be prolonged, although my body ached for a reprieve from the constant rigors of traversing nearly 30 kilometers a day. Tears of accomplishment welled in my eyes upon seeing the spires of the cathedral for the first time, and my thoughts swirled around the many days and countless steps that had finally delivered me to my goal.

What had I learned so far?

- Worrying about the future is useless. The only thing we are empowered to work with is the now.

- The physical body simply obeys what you tell it. If you tell it that it is inadequate, then it will perform inadequately. If you tell it that its potential is unlimited, then you get unlimited experiences

151

of physical output. If you tell it that it's too old, then it performs weakly. If you tell it that it keeps improving with age, then it does. Pure and simple.

- Whatever I may lack in speed I certainly make up for in stamina.

- I am polymorphic—no one thing at all times nor is anything ever set in stone. Some days I am an introvert, some days I am filled with extroverted tendencies. Some days certain walking styles will work, some days they won't. Some days I feel strong, some days I don't. None of it is right or wrong, it just is.

- Regardless of cultural heritage, people are the same all over the world. They want to be seen and heard. They want to feel safe and find their tribe of acceptance. They want to do things that expand their quests for meaning and they want to feel that they matter.

- Creature comforts are certainly wonderful *and* sometimes they hinder the deeper experience.

- No one can or will give me what I am unwilling to give myself.

Standing in front of that majestic cathedral, the one constructed over the bones of Saint James, I then did what every pilgrim before was encouraged to do—I took off my pack and lay on the ground to look up at the towering spires of the legendary holy place from a different vantage point.

This signifies that the pilgrim has now mastered seeing the world from a different perspective.

It was a beautiful day and the late morning sun was positioned directly behind one of the cathedral spires offering amazing back lighting. I lay on the stone of the plaza, stared up, and breathed—deep inhales of gratitude for my safe arrival, for life, for everything—and felt grateful for this particular spot on earth that had absorbed the relief and tears of countless pilgrims throughout the ages, grateful for being willing to die over and over again so that I could learn the art of living.

1) When reflecting on your own history of comparison and worry, what realizations, pivotal events, or memorable circumstances brought you to an expanded awareness that these traits carry no value?

2) The phrase *solution already exists* implies that everything we seek has already been created and waits for our realization of it. How do you welcome this in your life?

3) For those solutions that already exist, describe how you would set upon a course of action to go and meet them rather than deny their possibility.

4) What "deaths" are you ready to let happen and how will you begin to allow that release for yourself?

In the Meantime

> If we surrendered to earth's intelligence we could
> rise up rooted, like trees.
>
> — Rainer Maria Rilke

An infinitesimal seed starts to squirm and gyrate as the first tentacle of life pushes at its casing and breaks free. It thrusts the earthen walls away with its determined rise and is gifted for its efforts with an above-the-ground welcoming of sunlight and dew. It continues upward, unfolding with rapid motion to form bud, then fingerling petals, swiftly unfurling to showcase its flowering destiny. And we are privileged to see it all through the wonders of time-lapse photography.

Watching nature through this technique is like watching the product of faith occur within real time—an immediate illustration of seed to flower without hesitancy. The photographer takes a sequence of still images and then plays them back at multiple frames per second. It speeds up the real world in a way that you can't see with the human eye and works best with subjects that are moving at a slow pace.

We watch nature do its thing without constraint, resistance, or fear.

I've often wondered how we as spiritual beings having this human experience might benefit from watching our own evolution using this same technique. What if the camera was positioned on us? Shot after shot is taken over a lifespan and then, one day, we watch as those image sequences are sped up to reveal our years of growth, time-lapsing into a few series of seconds.

I first became fascinated with the spiritual benefits of such an idea after watching this technique used by a young man who edited his own self-portrait photographs (selfies) from the time he was twelve to his present age of nineteen. You saw the physical growth, the change in hairstyle, the emergence of facial hair, and the wide variety of clothing styles and expressions all within a matter of ninety seconds. Now with firsthand experience of his entire teenage years behind him, I wonder what the nineteen-year-old version might say, if possible, to assure his twelve-year-old version that he would make it through those next seven years. If he was bullied, could he accept with certainty that life was worth living and know it would get better? If he were the product of a broken home, would he be willing to consider that the experience, regardless of how painful at the time, would birth within him a sense of self-reliance that would shape the rest of his life in a positive way?

I take this same wondering and imagine what my future self might share with my present self or what my present self might share in the realm of comfort and wisdom to the much younger me. I would hope for something like this.

"There will never be any circumstance that can ever warrant the closing of your heart. Life is more provisional than personal. Learn to be fluid and do not cling to what was. There will never be anything worth the investment of retaliation, no matter how large the agreement from the populace. Learn to laugh, particularly at yourself. Worry will never be a profitable way to spend your time. Know there will never be a place on earth where the gift of you will not be enough. You will rise and you will fall, but from it all you will accept the choice to thrive, for a well-lived life, you'll discover, is exactly that, a choice. Relax. Enjoy your undeniable intelligence."

In 2010 American author and media pundit Dan Savage created the video campaign phenomenon known as the *It Gets Better Project*. Approximately 50,000 plus videos were created by people reaching out to the lesbian, gay, bi-sexual, transgender (LGBT) youth of our world in response to the startling rise of teen suicide due to bullying. The video creators' message was uniformly simple: "It gets better." To think that any present pain is the indicator of what the rest of life must be is deeply mistaken. Yet when any of us have been "in it"—the seeming quicksand of pain and anguish—there seems little to no hope of things ever regulating. But they can and most likely do if we let them. And the things that felt catastrophic and soul-numbing have a way of drifting away like dust clouds with the winds of change.

I recently married. If you were to read that sentence without knowing much about me, there would be nothing of unusual significance within the sentence. People marry all the time. As a gay man, however, the concept is still a relatively fresh one and marriage equality is continuously finding its footing across the globe as the new normal. I imagine that if this paragraph is read many years from now, readers might shake their heads in a sort of bemused fashion, unable to conceive of a time when this was not a natural part of society. The same can be said for many other events regarding equality, technology, and education. I pause and reflect on those years and can only smile a "but of course" smile of realization for how this once unheard of opportunity for someone of my orientation could have come to pass. Imagine what the ten-year-old version of me would have felt if my present day version could have sat down with him and shared what was to be. That ten-year-old, like countless others, was tormented over what he was feeling. My religious environment spoke fervently of the evils of such thoughts and the formulating seed of my being was not surrounded by one granule of hospitable soil. And yet, here I am. The container of my years of pushing through the soil to reach my present state of maturity introduced me to others who would help dissolve that torment. Thankfully, I kept going, doing my best, whether consciously or unconsciously, to allow the seed of my being to continue growing uninterrupted. The world and its collective consciousness are evolving. Today I am married to my husband Ty and our wedding ceremony was performed by none other than my first mentor and teacher, Louise Hay. I strongly feel that the collective mental work around these changing events will take them out of the *supernatural* and make them simply natural.

Just as in nature, our inbred intelligence wants to participate in our unfolding without the influence of hesitation or doubt. It wants to tell us to relax. It wants to tell us it only gets better. Just as a seed unaffectedly arrives at the formation of a plant, so are we designed to go from the seeds of our desires to their rightful manifestation. Given this, we begin to comprehend why so many philosophers and sacred texts deemed nature to be our greatest teacher. The book of Matthew reads, "And why take ye thought for raiment? Consider the lilies of the field, how they grow; they toil not, neither do they spin."

To sum it all up, those lilies grow, bloom, and even wither without apprehension.

Throughout our lives we are engaged in this same process, this cycle of creating. We are designed to desire for we are designed to evolve. Call it what you will, this desire, longing, or wanting is an innate energy of propulsion pulling us to travel the infinite range of experience that life offers any willing explorer. And it is within this sequence, from desire to demonstration, where the quality of a person's life is formed.

I call this sequence "in the meantime." Our ability and our willingness to simply know that all things are working together for our good *in the meantime* (from desire to demonstration) is life's main objective. It is our time to give birth to an already-having-received attitude.

In the meantime is the path of faith and, some would add, the path of developing courage. Yet what has always fascinated me personally is how nature does not need faith or courage. There are no "finding your life purpose" or "overcoming obstacles" workshops for the flora and fauna crowd. They *know* their purpose. These elements of nature grow without self-doubt. They do not debate their legitimacy or compare themselves to another. Our human selves must cultivate faith. Our human selves must cultivate courage. For example, in our infancy, nothing dilutes our inbred nature to stand even though up to this time we have only managed to crawl. We do not refer to babies as courageous when they repeatedly attempt to gain a sense of balance and walk after falling countless times. It is simply what babies are designed to do. It is instinct. Are we as adults any different? Are we not designed to do the same? Do we have an instinct to stand up and move forward when we fall? We each have had our share of emotional collapse—the pain of failure, the humiliation and embarrassment of "falling on our face." This falling never need be permanent nor does it erase the instinct to stand up again and continue moving forward. Yet when we as adults honor our instincts, we call these actions courageous.

Spiritual Scaffolding

In my many years of travel to Cambodia, I have continuously taken visitors to the ancient temple complex of Angkor Wat. During some of these first visits, the main entrance of this ancient wonder rested majestically, showcasing much of, what I imagine to be, its original splendor. In the subsequent years that followed, however, the monument's elevated towers and causeway have been surrounded by scaffolding. One can understand that restoration is a natural

160

part of reinforcing a lasting presence, but the intended goal of those doing the repairs is to one day take the scaffolding down.

I believe each of us is also a temple of sorts—a sacred sanctuary of inner knowing with a corresponding outer reflection.

Faith and courage are like spiritual scaffolding, a framework of support that we sometimes must erect around our lifestyles and daily practice to assist us in returning to the full restorative splendor of our souls' assignments. They are to be temporarily positioned, not permanently placed. To hold on to the necessity of faith or courage is to hold on to its opposing forces. If I must have more faith then I must be holding on to its opposing force of doubt. If I must live courageously then I must also be continuously relating to its opposing force of fear. How can I ever intend to align with the examples of our greatest teachers (nature and infants) if I never begin to dismantle the scaffolding—the belief in opposing forces—and thus begin honoring my instinctual knowing?

Take notice of your feelings around such questioning. Does the idea of moving beyond the need of courage and faith make you uneasy? Placing semantics aside, can you actively consider that anything less than a perpetual immersion of knowing can ever be your final destination regarding your soul's evolution? To be a willing vessel of universal mind and its infinite potential is to continuously place greater and greater seeds of intention and expansive desires into the eternally fertile soil of your *in the meantime*.

The Sandbox Paradox

Human reality would like to offer that life is a process. This perspective of *in the meantime* is experienced as something starting from an apparent nothing and hopefully becoming something. Spiritual reality would offer that everything already is. You and I create nothing for everything is already created. So this experience of *in the meantime* is more aligned with the removal of mental obstacles such as limiting beliefs or allowing shifts in perception so that we may reawaken to what already is. What we do, through our willingness, is uncover this creation. The beloved 13th century Persian poet Rumi said it masterfully: "Your task is not to seek love, but merely to seek and find all the barriers within yourself that you have built against it." So love then, according to Rumi, is already here, already around us.

So which *in the meantime* is the true one? Well, they both are according to our allegiance to them as truth. If reality was like an infinite, universal sandbox in which all life intermingled, then within this sandbox are two varying experiences, the life design of mankind and the life design from God-Cosmic Intelligence. This sandbox paradox describes well the dualism that permeates itself in a seemingly absurd, self-contradictory existence throughout humanity's perception.

Take the well-known idiom *There's a light at the end of the tunnel.* This is frequently offered as a statement of hope and we share it with others or even say it to ourselves to help bolster confidence or breathe wind back into our metaphoric sails, aiming to provide some semblance of comfort

162

in vulnerable times. It is offered as a promise to hopefully pacify a challenge and help one bridge any present level discomfort to a futurized resolve.

But what if the light that is referenced—the light representing the resolution of a current challenge—is not somewhere off in a yet-to-be determined future, but rather is surrounding us in this very moment?

What if the reality is this? The light is not at the end of the tunnel. The light is wherever you are. If you keep thinking your resolve lies in the future then it will always be just out of reach.

The recurring theme throughout the book has been an invitation to reexamine the way you perceive the world.

Consider

- that where you are right now, regardless of the circumstance or personal history, the truth of you in this immediate moment is as a being of wholeness.

- that because your solution already exists, worrying about any outcome is a waste of your time and energy.

- that life continuously extends support to lift you up into greater degrees of conscious awareness. You simply must surrender your control of the how and grab hold of the hand of solution and let it restore you to a place of realization.

- that your personal hell is a choice as is your personal heaven. Since you've often heard "you can't serve two masters," then which state of mind will you choose?

- that your pain is not special and by continuing to hold it as such robs you of the very freedom your inherent nature wants to return you to. As you let the attachment to the pain go, you let go of the self-imposed shackles that prevent you from moving forward.

- that gratitude will heal all sorrow, all guilt, all anguish, all fear. Being grateful for every event you encounter replenishes the power you have mistakenly given away.

- that by approaching life with a beginner's mind you reawake from a stagnant existence.

Through this willing examination of perception, we arrive at a new crossroads in consciousness. We stand on a new metaphoric patch of grass and have the opportunity to say that it *is* green, it *is* verdant, it *is* enough in this very moment. We make our next choices about our careers, our health, our relationships, our abundance. Those natural desires for what's next also come with the awareness that the fulfillment of those desires are not only fully formed, but are just as eager to meet us as we are to meet them.

We start in this moment to live our lives from these three basic decisions.

1) *Decide whether you want to live in God's world or the human world.*

The reality of God's world reveals there is always enough. The virtues you have come to equate with God are also the virtues within you, for all beings are a part of that which is Source itself. These qualities—wisdom, power, harmony, prosperity, love—reverberate within all beings awaiting their expression through personal permission. The poet Rumi also reminded, "You are not a drop in the ocean but the entire ocean in a drop."

It is here you come to understand the folly of concern. Your true nature knows you have already won. You are already a success. Your being is eternal and there is no shortage of good. You simply must claim these truths, even in their apparent absence, for the absence is only perception. You hold in your hand a cosmic net of sustenance woven from pure strands of unshakeable truth, constantly catching that which you need when you need it. Concerns are like vapor. You no longer waste any more of this life trying to catch and gather our concerns. You let them pass through the net unafraid.

2) *Decide to see with your mind rather than your eyes.*

To see with your mind is to conceive the infallible probability of what you desire. Whatever seed you place in the soil of this desire must grow. Your world is not confined by physical barriers, recorded history, genetic misfortunes, cultural customs, or your own past mistakes. Seeing with your mind is living from vision and the book of Proverbs

165

reminds us that where there is no vision, the people perish. To perish is to give in to the false perception that scarcity is possible, that others can and will take what rightfully belongs to you and that your world teeters on the possibility of failure and demise. Vision takes you to the threshold where the gifts of Spirit stand eager to enter into your reality. Vision helps you invite them in. These gifts are distributed unto you for you have prepared the place in your mind for them to be received. You now have the gift of wisdom, the gift of healing, and the gift of power. You have the gift of insight and holy communication.

To see with your mind is to gain the understanding that your soul's existence and your gifts are eternal. Death is a misconception, a false idea created by seeing with the eye rather than the mind. The eye sees this as final but the mind knows of the spiraling upward of consciousness upon which each soul continues.

3) *Decide to be progressive, not consistent.*

Knowing who you really are and establishing what world you reside in, begin now to live your life from a leading edge sensibility. Think of yourself as the vessel through which God expresses.

As a vessel of infinite potentiality, how will you establish relationships with the world around you? To be progressive is not to wither in an atmosphere of tried and true. Regardless of what others may say, your calling is to herd your own conformity out of the darkened corners of work, family, communication, organizations, religiosity, not with a judgmental force but simply by the power of your conscious presence. The power of your presence does not entertain divisive conversation, tactics of blame, or the fear of change. You are willing to trade history for mystery and know that the vital expansion of your soul's assignment awaits in the continuing yet-to-be. Deciding to be progressive is to let go of the manmade concept of security. Wherever you go, whatever the locale of your future years, you will always be the vessel of God. And you know that wherever God is, all is well.

1) If you had the opportunity to sit with your younger self and offer your present day wisdom, what would be some of the highlights you would share? In one sentence, what would be the overriding theme of that conversation? If in the future you were given the chance to sit with the present day you, what could you envision are the highlights of that conversation? What would the theme of that conversation be? How are the themes different, if at all?

2) What parts of your belief system are comparative to the instinctual actions of nature and infants—areas where you simply know that all things are working together for good?

3) Have you ever dismantled the scaffolding of faith and courage and felt restored in any area of your life? What parts of you are still residing upon faith and courage to get you through situations? What opposing force of faith (doubt) still lingers within you? What opposing force of courage (fear) still lives freely in your thoughts?

4) Name the steps you could begin to incorporate in your life with regard to a) living in God's world, b) seeing with your mind rather than your eyes, and c) being progressive, not consistent.

Afterword

Often while driving, I play an imaginary game I've called Deliberate Dialogue/Monologue. I pretend that I am being interviewed by various sources such as National Public Radio or Oprah's Life Class. The questions range from talking about my writing, to my non-profit work in Cambodia, to such broad philosophical topics as living a life of quality, the experience of death, and our eternal journey. Sometimes the dialogue morphs into acceptance speeches where I am being rewarded for my philanthropic aspirations in overseas education through grant monies. I thank the many out there who recognize and honor the work I am involved in with such profound and welcomed support. I do the same with my spiritual center where I am the minister, continuing the exercise by offering speeches of gratitude to the myriad supporters who have funded our programming and made it possible for us to share our vision of reawakening all to their spiritual magnificence.

It is a stimulating and conscious way for me to work with the use of the creative process, sending enthusiastic, initiated thought into the fertile, receptive energy of the subconscious. I love it so much that I have begun to even enjoy traffic congestion as it furthers my "interview" time where my imagination knows no bounds and global support is constantly flowing.

This mental game reminds me that any normalized activity can become sacred practice if we choose to make it so.

Throughout my journey of widely varying lessons, one theme continuously rises to the top of my list: life consists of one continuous opportunity to choose. When I was unconscious of the power of choice, the power of choice still operated and delivered to me the mental equivalent of my choosing. When I stumbled into a spiritual path of awareness, I saw that I had to *choose* a better result before I could ever *expect* a better result. I had fun in creating the following tongue twister to describe this process.

What becomes comes from being one with what becomes before it comes.

The yet to be is based on my being in alignment with the yet to be.

Within the lessons and stories offered in this book, it has been my intention to place a spotlight on that power of choice and invite everyone to consider that the deepest longings of our hearts begin their migration to us through our mental acceptance of their reality. We must learn to relish the idea that in this very moment, the grass is greener right here. Our hearts' desires are right here. Our long anticipated relief and freedom is right here because God, the Divine expression of Infinite Creation, is all that is in every moment.

We must choose this as our mental template if a loving existence is to be ours.

Love knows only love. We often say that God is love so from that we may deduce that God knows only God. Whatever your definition of God, It simply knows you as Its divine expression. It does not know you as marginal. It does not know you as wounded or disastrous. God knows only God. God knows the world and all its inhabitants as instruments of love.

We might choose to argue with this premise considering the blatant facts and actions of many across our world. Yet it is our perceptions that hold such an ideal in place.

Long ago, in a pizza restaurant I visited, stood a wall where people were encouraged to write. It was covered from floor to ceiling with people's names and dates plus drawings and doodles of everything imaginable. From my vantage point in the booth next to this wall was scribbled

God is love
Love is blind
Ray Charles is blind
Ray Charles is God

I remember laughing out loud and thinking to myself, "how true!"

Love knows only love. God knows only God. God knows only you as Its divine handiwork. You and I are God in expression. The only thing to determine is how much of my God nature I am deliberately expressing.

Perhaps it is time to begin a Deliberate Dialogue with this version of you. What would it be like to be in conversation with your power, your resilience, your endless stream of creative ideas and their rewarding effects? In this conversation, how might you describe your life and its transformation from lack to unlimited? What would it be like to be interviewed regarding your victories and life-enhancing achievements?

In one of my pretend interviews, I imagined what I would say if I were asked, "What would be your final words when departing this existence?"

They sounded something like this.

Everything will turn out just fine. In fact it will be more than fine. Your journey will be the journey you decide it to be and each of us will continue spiraling upward in awareness and adventure. There is nothing to be afraid of for nothing will ever separate you from the inclusive nature of the One. Along the way you will travel through the energies of pain, sorrow, joy, bewilderment, happiness, grief, fulfillment, satisfaction, and more. Not once will you be abandoned. You will become more conscious in your response to each of these feelings and you will learn to allow them to pass through you without resistance or judgment.

You will continue elevating yourself to more fulfillment, more joy, and more impactful periods of peace. Your fear of death is unwarranted for you do not die. We transition to another adventure but we do not die. So let that one go. By doing so you will begin to learn how to live, really live. You will travel this world with unshakeable knowing. Yes, please understand that everything will turn out just fine.

Blessed be,

David Ault
November 2014

Acknowledgments

My heartfelt thanks to my spiritual community, Spiritual Living Center of Atlanta in Atlanta, Georgia, for graciously offering me a platform, week after faithful week, to share, apply, and learn a philosophy of life-affirming principles. I am grateful for the continuing opportunity to be both teacher and student.

Additional thanks to

~ my staff at Spiritual Living Center of Atlanta: David Aurilio, Nathan Blankenship, Penelope Willams, plus the innumerable talent that selflessly serves our community. You are the embodiment of ideal support.

~ my editor, Nanette Littlestone, who cradled my words with the greatest respect. I am honored to have your energy in this work.

~ my ever-faithful life tribe who mindfully love and learn alongside me: Mark Wyrick, Tracey Owens, Tony DiStefano, Karen Drucker, Hope Perello. You are my heart.

~ my husband, Ty Andrews, for jumping into the adventure of the ever-changing waters of relationship. Thank you for your devotion to love and cherish one another come what may.

About the Author

David Ault is an internationally known author and celebrated metaphysical teacher and speaker. He is an ordained minister through Centers for Spiritual Living and currently serves as the Senior Minister of Spiritual Living Center of Atlanta in Atlanta, Georgia. His weekly messages are heard and viewed by thousands across the world.

Since his spiritual reawakening in the mid-1980s, Ault has traveled the globe offering his gifts as a singer/songwriter, speaker, and facilitator. He has established a thriving non-government regulated school in Siem Reap, Cambodia, which provides free education, medical/hygiene assistance, and agricultural and life skills training to hundreds of Cambodian children annually. He also offers humanitarian service trips there regularly. His stateside nonprofit, Khmer Child Foundation, serves this initiative.

David lives with his husband Ty Andrews in Atlanta, Georgia.

To learn more about David Ault visit:
http://www.davidault.com
http://www.khmerchildfoundation.org
http://slca.com

Made in the USA
San Bernardino, CA
07 November 2014